edacious

Samuel Johnson after Deconstruction

Rhetoric and *The Rambler*

Steven Lynn

Southern
Illinois
University
Press
•
Carbondale
and
Edwardsville

Library of Congress Cataloging-in-Publication Data

Lynn, Steven, 1952–
    Samuel Johnson after deconstruction : rhetoric and the Rambler /
Steven Lynn.
        p.   cm.
    Includes bibliographical references and index.
    1. Johnson, Samuel, 1709–1784—Technique. 2. Rambler (London,
England : 1750) 3. Rhetoric—1500–1800. 4. Deconstruction.
I. Title.
PR3537.T4L96   1992
824'.6—dc20   91-4951
ISBN 0-8093-1770-2   CIP

The paper used in this publication meets the minimum requirements of
American National Standard for Information Sciences—Permanence
of Paper for Printed Library Materials, ANSI Z39.48-1984. ∞

For Annette

Contents

Acknowledgments

I want first to thank Karl Beason for getting me started in general and George Brauer for introducing me to the eighteenth century. W. R. Keast enticed me to think about Johnson, and James Garrison and James Kinneavy gave crucial guidance in the early stages of this project. Other friends and colleagues have given me valuable advice on various portions of this book, sometimes without knowing it, and I would like to thank them by naming some: Eve Tavor Bannet, Greg Jay, Paul Korshin, Bill Matalene, Carolyn Matalene, Bill Rivers, Don Siebert, Meili Steele, Patrick Scott, Phil Sipiora, Bill Thesing, and John Trimble. John Burke, John Vance, and Jasper Neel read the entire manuscript and provided detailed suggestions and encouragements. John Burke also read a much earlier, much longer, and much different version; for his rigorous reading I am particularly indebted.

Unlike Johnson, I have had the good fortune to write "under the shelter of academick bowers." George Geckle, Joel Myerson, Trevor Howard-Hill, and Carol McGinnis Kay have been as supportive as any faculty member could wish administrators to be. I also want to acknowledge research and travel grants from the University of Alabama and the University of South Carolina, as well as a generous fellowship from the Folger Library that allowed me to attend Hans Aarsleff's seminar series and do extended research at that wonderful resource. And I very much appreciate the vision and guidance of Curtis Clark and Carol Burns at Southern Illinois University Press and the copyediting of George Nicholas.

Acknowledgments

Although most of this book has been written in smooth open water, it has been through some of life's rapids and eddies: for paddling with me, I want to thank my family: Ben and Leora, Dot and Chet, and all my brothers and sisters, congenital and acquired. Finally, I want to thank Annette, the love of my life. I am continually surprised and inspired by her strength, humor, and patience.

Portions of this book are based on material that has appeared elsewhere, and I thank the various publishers listed below for their permissions. For some of the last section of chapter 2, I have drawn on "Sexual Difference and Johnson's Brain," *Fresh Reflections on Samuel Johnson*, ed. Prem Nath (Troy: Whitston, 1987), 123–49; and on a review of Harold Bloom's *Dr. Samuel Johnson and James Boswell*, which appeared in *South Atlantic Review* 55 (May 1990): 143–46. Much of the second section of chapter 3 appeared in "Locke's Eye, Adam's Tongue, Johnson's Word: Language, Marriage, and 'The Choice of Life,' " *The Age of Johnson* 3 (1990): 35–61. That essay also provided a bit of the conclusion. The third section of chapter 3 contains some traces of "Locke and Beccaria: Faculty Psychology and Capital Punishment," *Executions and the British Experience from the Seventeenth to the Twentieth Century: A Collection of Essays* © 1990 by William Thesing with permission of McFarland & Company, Inc., Publishers, Jefferson, North Carolina 28640. This essay appeared first as the Joiner Prize essay in *Postscripts* 5 (1988): 1–12, the journal of the Philological Association of the Carolinas, and I am especially grateful to the PAC. Some material in chapter 4 is taken from "Johnson's *Rambler* and Eighteenth-Century Rhetoric," *Eighteenth-Century Studies* 19 (1986): 461–79.

Samuel Johnson
after Deconstruction

1

Introduction:
Johnson upon His Bedside,
after Deconstruction

> Whatever we experience, we find Johnson has been
> there before us, and is meeting and returning home
> with us.
>
> —W. Jackson Bate, *Samuel Johnson*

Shortly after the *Rambler* essays began to appear, Mrs. Samuel Johnson reportedly told her husband, "I thought very well of you before; but I did not imagine you could have written anything equal to this" (Boswell 1:210). Tetty Johnson has not been remembered for her critical acumen; if we think of her at all, it is most likely in the terms of Garrick's portrait: "very fat, with a bosom of more than ordinary protuberance, with swelled cheeks of florid red, produced by thick painting, and increased by the liberal use of cordials; flaring and fantastick in her dress, and affected in both her speech and behaviour" (Boswell 1:99). But Johnson, Boswell tells us, had "great confidence" in Tetty's "judgment and taste" (1:210), and he later agreed that these essays exhibited a remarkable concentration of his powers: "My other works are wine and water," he said to Samuel Rogers, "but my *Rambler* is pure wine" (Rogers 10).

This judgment, by perhaps the eighteenth century's least and most authoritative critics, was shared by many in Johnson's day.

Even though *London, The Vanity of Human Wishes,* and *Irene* had appeared, *The Rambler* most definitively established Johnson's fame. One indication of the series' impact is that during his lifetime Johnson was more often referred to as "the author of the *Rambler*," "Mr. Rambler," or even "Rambling Sam" than by any other epithet (Greene, *Updated* 104). Modern readers, who (like their eighteenth-century counterparts) tend to measure every essay series by the unparalleled success of *The Spectator*, may easily underestimate the significance of *The Rambler* when they learn that its initial printing never surpassed five hundred copies for any particular issue, compared to the thousands for *The Spectator*.[1] By almost any measure except that of Addison and Steele, however, *The Rambler*'s initial circulation was healthy, and its audience steadily expanded. As R. W. Wiles has shown, the provincial newspapers and urban monthly magazines often reprinted *Ramblers*. Since they could print whatever they liked, such piracy indicates Johnson's appeal. Indeed, we know that one essay was even stolen by a French publication and then noticed by an English editor who, unaware of its origin, translated it back into English (Boswell 1:356). The series, in other words, was no doubt more popular at first than its author realized, and as its popularity increased it was never out of print during Johnson's lifetime, enjoying at least ten editions. For a large collection of didactic essays, even in an age when the publication of sermons was sometimes profitable, the success of *The Rambler* is indeed impressive.

If Johnson, his contemporaries, and even Tetty acknowledged *The Rambler*'s greatness, and if it is a major work by a major figure and arguably the masterpiece of one of our greatest writers, at the center of the eighteenth century chronologically and intellectually, then we might well expect, especially given the enormous and expanding interest in Johnson in recent decades, that *The Rambler* would be the subject of an outpouring of critical attention in our day. In fact, we have seen important and innovative studies. But Donald Greene's observation in 1970, that "analytical study in depth of [*The Rambler*'s] contents has not yet been attempted" (*Johnson* 139–40), still remains surprisingly accurate today. As Paul Korshin lamented in 1984, *The Rambler* "has never been the subject of a book of any sort, to say nothing of a scholarly work" ("Conceptions" xvii). Most Johnsonians would agree, I think, that no more than a dozen truly outstanding studies have appeared. By considering what might account for this relative neglect of Johnson's greatest work (by his own estimation at least), we may be able to begin to see how we are in a position today, after deconstruction, to appreciate the series more.

Philip Davis's recent book, described on its dust jacket as "a challenging reading of the *Rambler* essays and *Rasselas*," illustrates particularly well one way that attention to the series typically is deflected. Davis's reading of the essays immediately becomes a far-ranging meditation on what they reveal of Johnson personally. Invoking the same sort of freedom, Davis says, that a novelist uses to create a character (8), his book finally is "an attempt imaginatively to incorporate Samuel Johnson within life now" (46), verging toward Davis's own autobiography, as he says in his acknowledgments. *In Mind of Johnson* thus becomes an especially self-conscious instance of what might be called, in honor of Boswell's constant use of the honorary title Johnson himself eschewed, the "Doctor Johnson" syndrome—the focus on Johnson rather than his works, on character (or often caricature) rather than writing. As John Burke puts it, Johnson is "a victim of his biography's success" ("Unknown" 3)—a complaint of course, as Burke points out, that Johnsonians have made for decades. The fault, however, according to Korshin, is not Boswell's, for his *Life* is "only one-third Boswell's biographical narration and two-thirds Johnson's correspondence and writings, specimens of conversation, and scholia" ("Paradox" xvi). Instead of blaming Boswell, who gives us an anthology of Johnson, Korshin says, we should blame our own "fascination" with "his biography, his biographers, and the tensions among them," for that fascination, not Boswell, "has absorbed such a great proportion of scholarly energy" ("Paradox" xvii). Whomever we blame, though, the effect is the same, as our attention continues to shift to Johnson's life. Korshin himself has recently offered a brief demonstration of how "an understanding of Johnson's intellectual development, as we can glean it from close scrutiny of *The Rambler* for 1751, helps to enlarge our knowledge of his life in that year" ("Conceptions" 301). Korshin's analysis is revealing, but its goal, we must note, is an understanding of Johnson's life, not *The Rambler* itself, which remains a source for biography.

One can hardly wish, however, that Johnson be less fascinating; besides, this biographical distraction does not fully account for *The Rambler*'s critical treatment. Certainly, the series poses some significant critical problems, perhaps most obviously in its expanse: three volumes, 1088 pages, in the Yale edition; 208 essays—all but 4, and parts of 3 others, amazingly, written by Johnson, who at the same time happened to be constructing one of civilization's great intellectual achievements, his *Dictionary of the English Language*. Sometimes attacked in Johnson's and subsequent ages for their difficult style, the essays are linguistically rather demanding, perhaps reflecting (it is often remarked) his lexicographical involvement—although Rhea Keast's challenge to translate any sesquipedalian Johnsonian sentence into a more concise form without loss of meaning, for decades defeated participants in his Johnson seminars (Johnson himself, to be sure, did declare and substantiate that his *Ramblers* could be improved).[2]

At any rate, one cannot breeze through them. In fact, their initial appearance, biweekly from Tuesday, 20 March 1750, to Saturday, 14 March 1752, probably marks out a reasonable pace for readers. Surely Johnson realized—especially given his own reading habits ("I have read few books through," he told William Bowles)[3]— that the notion of proceeding through the series, from 1 to 208, would be a hypothetical ideal, apt to occur only in exceptional instances. Even if he did not envision *The Rambler*'s representation in various anthologies of English literature, of eighteenth-century literature, and of his own writings, he surely would have recognized that most readers would be sampling his *vin pur*, not imbibing the whole thing. How has the practice of reading the essays individually and in selections affected the series' reception? How has Johnson's achievement been depicted?

Perhaps the most obvious thing to say is that some essays clearly cannot be appreciated individually. For example, number 37 is a continuation of the essay on pastoral poetry begun in number

36; number 170 is the first part of the mournful tale of a prostitute, concluded in number 171; numbers 186 and 187 tell the outrageously pitiful story of two Greenland lovers. If these issues should be presented together, what about numbers 86, 88, 90, 92, and 94, which all deal with Milton? In Brady and Wimsatt's *Samuel Johnson: Selected Poetry and Prose*, only number 94 appears. Reading this essay alone, which exposes Milton's faults in adjusting sound to sense, the reader may well conclude that Johnson adopts an unappreciative, nitpicky, and even hostile attitude toward Milton. We may get a different impression, however, from *Rambler* 90, where Johnson argues that in terms of versification, Milton "has performed all that our language would admit" (4:115). Of course, including all of the Milton criticism in a selection may give an unrealistic impression of the series as a whole. If one should decide to include the Milton sequence, then what about *Rambler* 93? Although it does not focus on Milton, it does consider whether criticism should be limited to pointing out beauties or may also properly point out faults—an issue clearly relevant to the Milton papers that surround it.

Johnson's narratives also are not limited to consecutive numbers. *Rambler* 132, for example, begins the story of the education of a nobleman, which is not completed until numbers 194 and 195. For Johnson's initial audience, this gap would have reflected the passage of time between the "letters"; it also would appear to suggest something about Johnson's view of his audience's memory and attention. To take another example, in *Ramblers* 113 and 115 Hymenaeus tells of his disastrous experiences in courtship; in *Rambler* 119 Tranquilla compares her experiences to his; and in *Rambler* 167 we find that Tranquilla and Hymenaeus have come together, as they announce their marriage. Although these four issues are clearly part of a whole, Donald Greene's *Samuel Johnson*, in the Oxford Authors series, prints only the first letter by Hymenaeus, and the concluding discussion of marriage by both Hymenaeus and Tranquilla. One need not be a radical feminist to see that such an omission alters the narrative. Most obviously, the anthology reader sees only part of the problems Hymenaeus has had finding a sensible woman, and we do not see the corollary problems that Tranquilla has had with men. It is easy to see why Greene would want to include at least some part of this sequence: it contains an extended consideration of marriage. Greene even places his two Hymenaeus and Tranquilla essays in a progression on that topic, calling them "marriage 3" and "marriage 4," as if they are linked to the discussion in *Ramblers* 18 and 39, which are presented as "marriage 1" and "marriage 2." One could argue that such a sequence, while pedagogically stimulating, is not Johnson's. Other readers might think that *Rambler 35,* which concerns "a marriage of prudence without affection," or particularly number 45, regarding "the causes of disagreement in marriage," are more fairly focused on "marriage" than *Rambler* 39, which deals with "the unhappiness of women, whether single or married" (to use the essays' traditional titles).

The anthologist faces other challenges in determining how to represent Johnson's achievement, because some essays, although not part of a narrative, are still overtly related: for instance, in *Rambler* 24 Johnson promises to deal with the religious implications of his topic, and he does so two weeks later, in number 28. Arguably, Johnson wants his audience to consider these two essays together, with some time for reflection in between. Is it then a mistake for Reid Stuart's anthology to include only *Rambler* 28? In number 175 Mr. Rambler situates his argument in the context of a point made "in a former paper." Interestingly, that paper appeared almost a year earlier in number 79. Should these two essays be considered together? Is *Rambler* 79 in a sense incomplete without number 175? In Bate's Yale selection of *Essays from the Rambler, Adventurer, and Idler*, the first essay appears but not the second. Did Johnson really expect his first audience to compare or connect the two?

These are in fact only the simpler problems involved with sampling *The Rambler*. As an undergraduate I was introduced to number 25, which was presented as an example of Johnson's position that we should err on the side of presumption rather than timidity. This essay is popular with anthologists, appearing in at least three of the most significant modern collections (Bronson; Bate; Chapman). Having invoked the example of Johnson for years to countenance boldness, I was then surprised by *Rambler* 81, which suggests we "err on the side of safety," and by *Rambler* 17, which urges us to "contract our designs." To do justice to Johnson's view(s), should an anthology contain all three essays? What about *Rambler* 29, which advises us to give in to neither hope nor fear, for reality is never as good or as bad as we imagine? Without some close reading, we cannot say that these essays are contradictory, but at the least they would appear likely to qualify and illuminate each other. Should the anthologist try to reflect (or create?) this sort of tacit conversation between such essays?

Furthermore, Johnson's initial audience—some of them at least—might reasonably have been expected to read more than two essays in succession. The various anthologies, however, include only two consecutive essays, or at most three (in Bate's generous Yale selection). Does Johnson work with some sort of continuity in mind—which is slighted by the emphasis on isolated essays? To put the question another way, is *The Rambler* a loose collection of mostly unrelated, autonomous essays that can be extracted from the series without significant loss? Or is there some significant relationship not only between content-related essays (however we distinguish these) but also between contiguous and proximate essays? Is the experience of reading successive essays important? When we read single essays, are we taking them out of context? If so, what is the context? What does "The Rambler" stand for? Is it singular or plural?

Such questions would seem to be especially crucial for anyone constructing a sample of *The Rambler*, or reading one. Selecting the best essays or the most typical essays would seem to require some notion of intention or coherence: "Best" for what purpose? "Typical" of what? *Rambler* 4 almost always appears in the various selections; in surveys of English or eighteenth-century literature, it may be the only example offered (Bredvold; Abrams, *Norton*) or at most one of two or three essays (Baugh; Moore). *Rambler* 60 is almost as popular with anthologizers. Why do these two essays appear so regularly? How do they represent *The Rambler*? *Rambler* 4 deals with popular fiction and is generally assumed to compare Fielding to Richardson. *Rambler* 60 is concerned with the art of biography, and

7

one "by-product" of Johnson's position, as Bate puts it (*Johnson* [1975] xix), is Boswell's *Life of Johnson*. Both essays, in other words, are important for reasons extrinsic to the series itself. To know if these essays, or any other selection of essays, are particularly representative of *The Rambler* as a whole in any sense, we would have to have some idea of the whole thing.

But the series as a whole is precisely what few people have ventured to think about at length. A. T. Elder concludes that the central theme of *The Rambler* is the importance of contributing to society. For T. F. Wharton it is "the dream of literary greatness" that "came almost inevitably to dominate the series" (57). J. C. Riely asserts that "the great theme" of Johnson's essays "follows the familiar teaching of Ecclesiastes that 'all is vanity and vexation of spirit' " (385). Bate sees *The Rambler* as a prose explication of *The Vanity of Human Wishes*, a religious poem, although "in the prose writing," Bate says, "the religious answer is in general implied rather than stated" (Johnson, *Rambler* 3:xxxii). What that implied religious answer comes down to is "the need for a fuller awareness and more enduring courage" (3:xxviii), which may seem only faintly religious. Paul Alkon also perceives a theological interest in the series, but he is unable to decide "whether the secular or the religious aspect . . . is, ultimately, the more noteworthy" (*Discipline* 178).

In addition to the distraction of Johnson himself, the bulk and complexity of the series, the difficulty of saying which essays are essentially related, the problem of what the series as a whole is about (if anything), and the consequent problem of determining a principle of selection or valuation, *The Rambler* would also appear to pose a methodological challenge. Although we currently inhabit a critical pluralism that seems at times to approach pandemonium, there is wide agreement that for much of this century most of our critical assumptions have been shaped by New Criticism.[4] It is far from clear how New Criticism, taking the lyric poem as its normative genre, should be applied to the essay—much less to an essay series. Throughout his career, to be sure, Johnson worked in genres resistant to the critic who seeks the ironies and paradoxes of a well-wrought urn: dictionary entries, prefaces, critical biographies, invented debates, sermons, law lectures, editorial decisions and comments, scattered epigraphs, various translations, deliberative poetry. No wonder biographical and historical projects, tracing Johnson's intellectual context or development, his psychological complexity, or the economic, marital, or social facts of his life, have been so appealing.

I think that one other factor, perhaps more important than the others combined, has affected serious study of *The Rambler*: few readers, I suspect, really expect the series to be all that good, to repay their closest attention. Even Walter Jackson Bate, Johnsonianissimus, quotes Johnson's assessment that his *Rambler* was "pure wine" and then immediately offers this confident correction of that view: "But he was really thinking of the best of them (though there are many good ones), for the series is naturally uneven" (*Johnson* 290). If Bate's reaction is at all typical, we can easily see why sensible persons go to one of the selections of essays, enjoying some of the truly "good ones" for now. Of course, we must recognize that no one, even Bate, can possibly know for sure what Johnson was "really" thinking. If Johnson did in fact say his series was "pure wine," it seems somewhat unlikely he actually meant it was in his estimation only partly wine, that only the best were wine. But rather than expose Johnson to the embarrassment of overvaluing his own work, we have assumed with Bate he cannot have said what he meant.

Obviously I do not wish to deny that the series is in some sense "uneven." Even the purest wines vary. My point is that Bate does not proceed to support his correction of Johnson's opinion by an analysis of particular flawed or weak essays. Instead, he turns immediately to the circumstances of Johnson's composing, telling us that "the *Rambler* essays were written more rapidly and with less leisure to outline, consider, or improve them than the works of any major moralist" and that many "were written without even being read over once" before being printed (290–91)—as if these facts alone (if they are facts) sufficiently illustrate the work's unevenness.

How *The Rambler*'s title has been perceived is a particularly revealing reflection of how the series as a whole has been viewed. According to Boswell, "The Rambler" was a "not very happy" choice (1:202), and his assessment has been echoed by generations of readers, even by Johnson's most ardent champions. James Clifford, for instance, says, "Even in our day many readers must keep wondering why Johnson finally chose the *Rambler*, a title which hardly describes the serious moral content of the essays" (73). And Bate, one of those readers wondering, judges in the *Yale Edition* that the title "seems singularly inappropriate for the kind of publication he had in mind" (Johnson, *Rambler* 3:xxii). One can almost see John Wain shrugging in his defense of Johnson's taste (if not his title): "For his part, [Johnson] never pretended that *The Rambler* was a good name" (152).[5]

When Wain says that Johnson never pretended his title was a good one, he is no doubt alluding to the story Boswell tells us that Reynolds told him that Johnson told *him* about how he (Johnson again) selected his title:

> What *must* be done, Sir, *will* be done: When I was to begin publishing that paper, I was at a loss how to name it. I sat down at night upon my bedside, and resolved that I would not go to sleep till I had fixed its title. *The Rambler* seemed the best that occurred, and I took it. (1:202)

This story obviously supports Boswell's dismissal of Johnson's title: it was chosen, we see, by a man eccentric enough to set an arbitrary deadline for selecting a title. Johnson sits on his bed and amusingly decides he must have a title before he can sleep. To get some rest he accepts "The Rambler," a title no one should take very seriously. It means "only," so Clifford says Johnson's readers "soon sensed," "shifting subject matter and not lack of serious commitment" (73). If the title does not really stand for anything in particular, then the reader is hardly encouraged to generate a serious commitment to the series, nor is it clear what the object of Johnson's "serious commitment" might be. Indeed, what is usually said about Johnson's motives in writing the series does not enhance our assiduity or our opinion of his. According to Thomas Tyers, his friend and contemporary, Johnson wanted to gain some "relief from his application to the Dictionary" (Hill 2:350), and he also desired, as Clifford puts it, "some other source of regular income" (73). Of course, Johnson's commitment was serious enough to produce the essays, but readers seem to keep returning, like Bate, to the manner of their production, noting that they were generally dashed off at the last second. Such procrastination is consistent with the whimsical title, a wandering intention, and mundane motivations. As Raman Selden says, *The Rambler* was "rather casual writing" (279).

Stories of origins are especially suspicious at this point in our critical history, and I want to return now to Boswell's (Reynolds's [Johnson's]) story of the origins of "The Rambler" in order to provide another starting point for engaging the series. Even if we assume that Johnson, Reynolds, and Boswell all remembered and reported accurately Johnson's bedside deliberation, we should notice the function this story plays in Boswell's self-presentation. Here is the sentence offering Boswell's judgment of Johnson's choice, setting the context for the Reynolds story:

> Johnson was, I think, not very happy in the choice of his title, *The Rambler*, which certainly is not suited to a series of grave and moral discourses; which the Italians have literally, but ludicrously, translated as *Il Vagabondo*; and which has been lately assumed as the denomination of a vehicle of licentious tales, *The Rambler's Magazine*. (1:202)

The caution of Boswell's "I think," disarming potential resistance to the presumption of his criticism, is dissolved by "certainly": if the title is "certainly" unsuitable, then Boswell hardly need qualify his assertion that the choice was "not very happy." The "which" clauses following this move appear to authorize Boswell's subordinate judgment, but in fact this support is beside the point. The ludicrous translation or the licentious appropriation may tell us something about translating English into Italian or marketing bawdy tales, and the anecdotes are indeed amusing, but they really do not tell us anything about the happiness of Johnson's title or the quality of his bedside deliberations.

Boswell attaches to the Reynolds story a footnote that makes even clearer its manipulative function. Garrick, Boswell tells us, once suggested that Edward Moore call his essay series "The Sallad" (1:202n.4). This note may appear to be no more than evidence of Boswell's effort to work in every anecdote he has collected (an effort for which Johnsonians mostly give thanks), until we see that it subtly reinforces the idea that Johnson's title is foolish. Other periodicals have had silly titles proposed for them, so we should not be surprised by "The Rambler." Johnson appears even more eccentric (comic and lovable also, to be sure), when we read that Moore, unlike Johnson, was not content with the fruits (or vegetables) of one night's effort, rejecting "The Sallad" and waiting patiently for Dodsley's considerably more ambitious suggestion, "The World." Boswell's note continues, somewhat surprisingly, to tell us that Garrick's proposal was "by a curious coincidence afterwards applied to himself" by Goldsmith in the lines "Our Garrick's a sallad, for in him we see / Oil, vinegar, sugar, and saltness agree." This hors d'oeuvre appears to go even further outside Johnson's or even Boswell's texts. But Boswell brings it in, I think, simply to associate Johnson's sleep-ransoming title with a whimsical verse, making us even more willing to smile at Johnson's title.[6] Boswell is constructing the mythic, odd, fascinating Johnson, at the expense of (the title of) his work.

As we might expect, there have been some attempts to account for, if not justify, how Johnson might have arrived at his silly title. The suggestion by Arthur Murphy, Johnson's contemporary, that "the title was most probably suggested by the *Wanderer*," has often been repeated. The close connection between "to wander" and "to ramble" in Johnson's *Dictionary*, where one is defined in terms of the other, lends some support to Murphy's suggestion. But Murphy certainly exaggerates when he says Savage's poem is discussed "with warmest praise in the *Life of Savage*" (Hill 1:391). Actually Johnson details the "universal" criticism of the poem: that "the disposition of the parts is irregular," the design "obscure," the plan "perplexed," the images "without order," and the whole performance "a heap of shining materials thrown together by accident" (*Lives* 2:365). Since this "criticism is universal," Johnson acknowledges that "it is reasonable to believe it at least in a great degree just" even though "Mr. Savage was always of a contrary opinion." Johnson is not enthusiastic about Savage's *Wanderer*, and I doubt that his title specifically alludes to or refers to that poem.

The suggestion has also been made that the title refers to the shifting subjects of the series, perhaps even to the shifting styles employed. At one point Boswell explains the "uniformity" and lack of variety in the series by reminding us that it was "entirely the work of one man" (which is almost accurate), but shortly thereafter he celebrates its "numerous subjects," "considerable portion of amusement," "fertility of fancy, and accurate description of real life," and "poetical imagery" (1:214–17). No doubt Johnson's title was designed to entice readers with the promise of variety, and the series does cover quite a range, from the announcement by Hermeticus of a magnet that detects infidelity (*Rambler* 199), for example, to the meditation on the lessons learned at a friend's deathbed (*Rambler* 54). Many of the serious essays are so powerful that it is perhaps easy, in retrospect, to think that only "grave and moral discourses" populate the series, forgetting perhaps such instances as the Swiftian essay on the advantages of living in a garret, the whimsy of the dream of a "universal register," or the sentimental mushiness of Anningait and Ajut's romance (*Ramblers* 117, 105, 186, and 187).

But the title has a much deeper resonance. Some two years after *The Rambler* ended, Johnson wrote to Thomas Warton that he saw himself as "broken off from mankind, a kind of solitary wanderer in the wild of life, without any certain direction, or fixed point of view. A gloomy gazer on a World to which I have little relation" (Boswell 1:277). Although Johnson connected this feeling to the loss of Tetty in 1752, it seems clear, as Bate and John Wain have most movingly shown, that Johnson viewed himself throughout his life—certainly going back to his brief time at Oxford—as an outcast, a wanderer without roots, a rambler. At age sixty-nine, so famous that it seemed the newspapers reported his every move, Johnson could still say: "I am a straggler. I may leave this town and go to Grand Cairo, without being missed here or observed there" (Boswell 3:306). Like his contemporaries, and like us, Johnson quite often thought of life as a journey, a voyage, a walk. So many of his own excursions, of course, seemed to have no particular goal, expressing simply a large desire to get out and see. They were more like his youthful trips on foot from Lichfield to Birmingham and back (some thirty miles of muddy road, to get control of his thoughts), than some purposeful travel to a fulfilling destination. He once asked Hester Thrale, "Was there ever yet any thing written by mere man that was wished longer by its reader, excepting Don Quixote, Robinson Crusoe, and the Pilgrim's Progress?" (Hill 1:332), and it is not surprising that his three favorite stories, excluding perhaps Scripture, dealt with searching wanderers, errant ramblers. "The Rambler," I will argue, points not only to Mr. Rambler and to Johnson, but also to the rest of us, who must also perpetually search for some meaningingful path in a confusing, chaotic world.

Such a claim can be supported of course only by looking at the series itself, and in a sense the rest of this study aims to show that Johnson thought more clearly and carefully upon his bedside than we have recognized and that this thoughtfulness continued throughout the writing of the essays. To frame and authorize such a reading, we need another starting point. For me *The Rambler* starts from Johnson's famous prayer composed at the outset of his project: "Almighty God, . . . without whose grace all wisdom is folly, grant, I beseech Thee, that in this my undertaking thy Holy Spirit may not be witheld from me, but that I may promote thy glory, and the Salvation both of myself and others" (*Diaries* 43). Johnson's controlling aim throughout *The Rambler*, I maintain, is exactly what he says here: to promote God's glory and "the Salvation of myself and others." This search—as I attempt to show by juxtaposing Johnson's skepticism and deconstruction and articulating his systematic view of the entropy of contentment and the endless return of desire—is in Johnson's estimation doomed. The searching itself is as much of the finding as we can securely obtain here, but this nothing, acutely perceived, may lead us to derive considerable comfort from our rambling in this world—if we choose intensely to strive to orient ourselves toward some transcendent Other.

Such is the posture Johnson assumes repeatedly throughout the series and emphatically at its conclusion. There Johnson identifies the four kinds of essays he has published, and he implicitly ranks them according to their religious impact. He virtually dismisses "the idle sports of the imagination," which have been "allotted few papers" since "it has been my principal design to inculcate wisdom or piety" (5:319). This design—overwriting the aim announced in the opening essay, "the entertainment of my countrymen" (3:7)—is singular: "wisdom or piety" does not offer alternatives but rather a second naming, "wisdom" and "piety" being finally the same, as the series has shown in many ways.

Next Johnson considers "the disquisitions of criticism," and his assessment seems to respond to the poststructural suggestion that criticism might become "creative as well as judicious," as the critic "overextends his art," in Geoffrey Hartman's words (215). Johnson turns away from this possibility, maintaining that criticism, "in my opinion, is only to be ranked among the subordinate and instrumental arts" (5:319). "Arbitrary decision and general exclamation" have been "carefully avoided" in his own judgments, he says, because his "principles" have been based on "unalterable and evident truth." Such a foundational declaration of faith may seem naive from our perspective. In practice, however, Johnson characteristically uses the hypostasis of "unalterable and evident truth" in an essentially deconstructive fashion, exposing the arbitrariness of various existing principles, pointing toward a foundation conspicuously absent. A brief look at Ramblers 156 and 158, one of Johnson's most revealing theoretical discussions of criticism, supports this suggestion.

In Rambler 156 Johnson compares the "close inspection" of criticism's illusions to two other actions: "the resuscitation" of the "first principles" of government and the restoration of bodily health "to the just equipoise which health requires" (5:65–66). The "origin" in these examples, to which we attempt to "return," is a heuristic device, a construct: we cannot go back to the moment of creation when our bodies were perfectly healthy, our government pure, our criticism fully grounded. Johnson perceives perfectly well that something apparently was already lacking at the start, or our governments and bodies would not be "perpetually degenerating towards corruption," nor our scholarship "perpetually tending to error and confusion." Attempting to return to a postulated origin means in effect, for Johnson, dismantling and clearing away "the accidental prescriptions of authority" (5:66). As he writes two essays later, reiterating his point, "the rules hitherto received" turn out, "upon examination," to be only "the arbitrary edicts of legislators" (5:76). Even in physiological terms, the movement toward reestablishing health involves a taking away, the removal "of the peccant humour" (5:65). For the literary critic, the act of looking toward some foundational origin, which can never be fully recuperated, reveals that "practice has introduced rules" (5:76) rather than vice-versa. The critic gains by losing when such arbitrary rules (the necessity of five acts in a play, the exclusion of tragicomedy for instance) are discarded.

It is perhaps easy not to notice that deconstruction actually depends upon the imagination of origins, of foundations, of "unalterable and evident truth," which any particular formulation can be shown to miss. One cannot expose "the logocentric error" unless one supposes logocentric belief. Or, as Paul de Man puts it, if deconstruction is perceived as "the recognition of the systematic character of a certain kind of error, then it would be fully dependent on the prior existence of this error" (*Allegories* 17). In his criticism Johnson is willing to venture "other rules more fixed and obligatory" (5:69) that seem almost minimalist by eighteenth-century standards: that in "every play the chief action should be single," and that a tragedy should "always have a hero" (5:70). Even these rules are not presented as fully "fixed and obligatory," but only relatively more secure, still subject to "close inspection" (5:66). Thus, Johnson's critical theory parallels, as we shall see in detail, his theory of life. Both involve orienting ourselves towards an origin, a foundation, which is a gesture that for Johnson involves us most immediately in exposing illusions of presence. Thus, establishing "principles of judgment on unalterable and evident truth" most often means in The Rambler disestablishing some falsely revered theory or practice. Likewise, turning his reader toward God typically means in practice most immediately confronting nothing, or no thing, turning away from what we (falsely) value.

The third category of *Ramblers*, "the pictures of life," are

16

ranked higher than the criticism, and these essays are more directly aimed at the reader's reformation. Johnson even avows that he has limited the "novelty" and "surprize" of his portraits to make them more realistic and hence more useful. Most directly didactic, of course, are the "essays professedly serious," in which Johnson takes the most pleasure. These essays, he says, "will be found exactly conformable with the precepts of Christianity, without any accommodation to the licentiousness and levity of the present age" (5:320). The other kinds of essays, which we may assume do represent some "accommodation," appear then to have been used to create readers for the "professedly serious" ones. By subtracting a substantial portion of his work, Johnson seems to purify his series, leaving himself in the posture toward which we are urged to struggle. Here are the final words of *The Rambler*, which Johnson adapts from Dionysius Periegetes, saving this pagan writer, finding the Logos in His absence:

> Celestial pow'rs! that piety regard,
> From you my labours wait their last reward.[7]

I am, then, taking most seriously what Johnson says both before the series began and at its end. Obviously, my method is not fully deconstructive. For one thing, there would seem to be little point in dismantling a text that is already perceived to be an essentially arbitrary collection of fragments—fragments that are themselves already the trace of a contradictory, associational, rambling logos. My goal instead is to (re)constitute Johnson's controlling evangelistic aim. Although I see the series as a coherent whole, a single symphony, my approach is also not New Critical but rather rhetorical—the analysis of aims, structures, strategies, and effects. In situating this rhetorical analysis "after deconstruction," I am acknowledging that these structures emerge from the possibility that they are there; without such a framing, which is itself always subject to exposure, we miss them. Deconstruction does not preclude the assertion of such intention and control, but rather requires it (in order to oppose it). Deconstruction, despite its heroic gyrations, does not in my view alter our thinking fundamentally, only

17

our evaluation of its results. What comes "after deconstruction," as Paul de Man, Terry Eagleton, Jonathan Culler, and others in various ways have noted, is rhetoric. *by which they do not mean what we*

How does a rhetorical analysis situated after deconstruction address the various obstructions to in-depth study of *The Rambler*? From such a perspective, Johnson himself is not a distraction from the text but a necessary construct for its analysis: the perception of structures and strategies and their effects stems from recognizing (inventing) Johnson's controlling intention. In this regard I find that trying to place Johnson's strategies within the context of his time is helpful. Therefore in chapter 3 of this book, Johnson's conception of time, space, and language (especially its origin as an indicator of its nature) figure importantly, and chapter 4 considers Johnson's position within the history of logic and rhetoric. Certainly, we can always expose the failure of Johnson's intention or our misreading of it. The more valuable and challenging task at this point, I think, is to chart its success.

Rhetorical analysis also allows me to deal with the series' bulk and complexity by relating selected essays to the strategy of the whole. Thus I have tried here to deal with a sufficient number of essays, both individually and sequentially, to make my argument plausible, not exhaustive or (I hope) exhausting. In designing *The Rambler* as a rhetorical instrument, Johnson has recognized that readers would encounter the essays in a wide variety of ways. The series is not itself a strictly linear argument, although reading the essays in succession, I suggest, is richly rewarding. Proceeding in whatever fashion, the reader experiences a series of repetitions, qualifications, reversals, and diversions that can be productively related to Johnson's aim. Johnson's strategy is designed for how real readers may encounter the series—reading straight through, reading parts in sequence, skipping about, forgetting, connecting and comparing in myriad ways. My second chapter therefore examines closely the opening four essays and also a significant number of other related ones. The third chapter continues this sequential and distributed analysis, looking at the next four essays as well as other ones throughout the series. The fourth chapter focuses on the question of sequencing within essays and throughout the series.

18

Look at pp. 16–18 for an interesting, not-so-subtle argument in defense of old-fashioned, conventional rhetorical analysis

If a rhetorical perspective bypasses some of the obstructions to *The Rambler*, what is the motivation for starting "after deconstruction"? For one thing, after we have seen rigorous readings of a postcard and a wrestling match, deconstruction does appear to authorize the close reading of any text. The idea of reading a neglected essay series closely, as if it were "literature," seems rather unremarkable. More importantly, "after deconstruction" is where we are today, inescapably. That is also where we find Johnson: for if deconstruction is a way of seeing or failing to see (a certain kind of particularly radical skepticism), then Johnson is an especially valuable resource today, for he seems after deconstruction pretty much to have been there before us, to be meeting us, and showing us how to return home—as Bate says he always is. From where we are, then, after deconstruction, some crucial features of Johnson's thinking, frequently observed by various readers (his tendency to think in dyadic terms, to contradict himself, to contradict anyone else, for instance), come into a different and perhaps helpful light. But my argument here is not (simply) that Johnson anticipates deconstruction, but rather that he also differs so profoundly and instructively from it.

Thus, my second chapter deals with an important deconstructive concept, misreading, especially as it is worked out by Harold Bloom, who is of course usually grouped with the Yale deconstructionists but who differs from Derrida in a crucial way that parallels Johnson's differing. Bloom's familiar vision of the anxiety of influence illuminates Johnson's strategies, but these strategies also expose Bloom's interest. My third chapter, bringing Johnson and Derrida together carefully (matter and anti-matter perhaps), considers the surprising presence and saving absence of a handful of deconstructive themes in Johnson, especially in *The Rambler*. My fourth chapter examines the movement of Johnson's thought, the *dispositio* of his discourse, which may be seen to work through a deconstructive vision—both by means of and toward some other insight.

But why, among things we may wonder at this point, if *The Rambler* is a religious work, is the Bible cited only 7 times in comparison to, say, 103 references to Horace or 37 to Juvenal? Partly because Johnson does not want to frighten off his largely secular audience. But mostly because his strategy in *The Rambler*, as I want to show, involves the reader in a process of education that is not by any means a direct and confident route to salvation (Johnson himself could not find such a way), but is instead a troubling, difficult, evasive, confusing, and especially rambling journey. Johnson could have cited chapter and verse, and he does so in his sermons. His way to such a mazing grace in the *Rambler* essays involves such struggle and indirection because he perceives so clearly the forces—logical, psychological, and emotional—that undermine and erode it. Such forces of skepticism and uncertainty, exposing the absence of any ultimately ordering Word, have arguably come together in our time most acutely in the project of deconstruction.

Therefore, after deconstruction, we may see more clearly what Johnson was up to, and his achievement in *The Rambler* may reveal more clearly what we ought to be up to, after deconstruction.

2

(Mis)Reading *The Spectator*: *The Rambler* in Bloom

Speaking of Homer, whom he venerated as the prince of poets, Johnson remarked that the advice given to Diomed by his father, when he sent him to the Trojan war, was the noblest exhortation that could be instanced in any heathen writer, and comprised in a single line:

Αἰὲν ἀριστεύειν, καὶ ὑπείροξον ἔμμεναι ἄλλων

which, if I recollect well, is translated by Dr. Clarke thus: *semper appetere praestantissima, et omnibus aliis antecellere.*

—William Maxwell qtd. in Boswell

"Johnson Had No Competitors"

According to Sir John Hawkins, when *The Rambler* first began to appear "Johnson had no competitors for applause; his way was open, and he had the choice of many paths" (261). This assessment by Johnson's friend and biographer is intriguing. For one thing, the announcement of Johnson's series in the *Gentleman's Magazine* indicates, as we might well expect, that he did have at least one immediate competitor: "Two new designs have . . . appeared about the middle of this month, one entitled, *The Tatler revived; or, The Christian Philosopher and Politician. . . .* The other, *The Rambler*" (March 1750; 20:126). Boswell, seemingly ever eager to triumph over Hawkins, does mention Johnson's "competitor for fame in the same form," but for once he does not point to Hawkins's oversight (1:201–2). If Hawkins did not recall (understandably enough) *The Tatler revived*, he was certainly aware of a host of other efforts to resurrect Addison and Steele's legendary successes. The question of how Hawkins could conclude that Johnson "had no competitors" is especially worth considering for what it may suggest about the way others, including Boswell and Johnson, viewed the context of the *Rambler*'s beginning.

When Hawkins turns in his biography to *The Rambler*, he first feels compelled to support the very decision by Johnson to work in the lowly genre of the essay ("What are the sapiental books in the Scriptures, and all collections of precepts and counsels, but moral essays?" [260]). He then seems to continue this defensive posture by observing that "a long space had intervened since the publication of the Tatlers, Guardians, and Spectators." Boswell similarly justifies Johnson's undertaking a periodical paper by linking it to "the *Tatler, Spectator*, and *Guardian*," which had enjoyed "great success" and which "were the last of the kind published in England" (1:201). Johnson chose this "vehicle" to appear as "a majestick teacher of moral and religious wisdom," Boswell says, because "such an interval had now elapsed since their [*Tatler, Spectator, Guardian*] publication, as made him justly think that, to many of his readers, this form of instruction would, in some degree, have the advantage of novelty" (1:201).

For Hawkins, the implication that it was time for another essay series, that *The Rambler* was warranted by this "long space," immediately requires some further explanation. "It is true," Hawkins must admit, that this "space" already "had been filled up by *The Lover*, and *The Reader, The Theatre, The Lay-monastery, The Plain-dealer, The Free-thinker, The Speculatist, The Censor*, and other productions of the like kind" (260–61). Boswell, however, who knows about *The Tatler revived*, which he quickly dismisses with the observation that it was "born but to die," seems surprisingly to know nothing about any other earlier imitations (Addison and Steele's work being "the last of the kind"), although he considerably qualifies the "novelty" he ascribes to Johnson's effort ("to many of his readers," and "in some degree").

What motivates these silences and spaces? To celebrate Johnson's series Hawkins obviously must distinguish it from the host of imitators. So he upholds the notion of a "space" after "the Tatlers, Guardians, and Spectators" by hastening to dismiss these revivals. Some "were nearly still-born," and the others "enjoyed a duration little more extended than that of the ephemeron" (261). Boswell also applies a fatal/fetal metaphor for the same reason, but to Johnson's immediate competitor rather than the intervening ones. However, even if there is really nothing (viable) left between the origin of the periodical and *The Rambler*, Hawkins still needs to maintain a "space" between them, attempting to evade the inevitable comparison that will necessarily point to the secondary status of Johnson's work, already suspect because of its genre. Hawkins needs, in a sense, to assert that Johnson had "no competitors" precisely because he had so many, both original and derivative. His declaration that Johnson's "way was open, and he had the choice of many paths" constitutes the denial of an inescapable contrary reality. Johnson, in more ways than one, could not avoid following after Addison and Steele. Boswell's silence also strives to overlook what is hidden in his qualifications of Johnson's novelty, namely, that others had preceded Johnson's imitation, the imitation of many imitations, which somehow nonetheless has to have "the advantage of novelty."

Hawkins seems himself to be aware that his strategy leaves something more to be said. "Add to this," he immediately goes on, "that a period of near forty years, in a country where commerce and its concomitant luxury had been increasing, had given rise to new modes of living, and even to characters that had scarcely before been known to exist" (261). Hawkins points for example to the clergyman who had become "an amphibious being," the "stately stalking fop" who had become "a fidgeting, tripping animal," the shopkeeper who had become a merchant, and the stockbroker who had become "a man of gallantry." Even if Johnson is bound to follow Addison and Steele (which Hawkins wants to deny), fashions and

23

morals have changed enough in forty years, Hawkins says, to justify updating the *Tatler*, *Guardian*, or *Spectator*. Likewise, Boswell, accounting for Johnson's initial lack of success, will later assert that his work was "distinguished . . . from other periodical papers" by Johnson's uniquely "grave and often solemn cast of thinking" (2:208).

Hawkins and Boswell are struggling to forestall exactly the sort of reaction Mary Wortley Montagu conveyed to the Countess of Bute: "The Rambler is certainly a strong misnomer. He allwais [sic] plods in the beaten road of his Predecessors, following the Spectator (with the same pace a Pack horse would a Hunter)" (3:65–66). Similarly, Catherine Talbot, one of Johnson's supporters, writing to Elizabeth Carter as the series first appeared, was happy to see Johnson trying more "papers of amusement," for "London swarms with what would afford as amusing subjects as any in the Spectator." But she soon was forced to conclude that "humour and the manners of the world are not his forte" (Carter and Talbot 1:348–49). In other words, Hawkins's odd assertion and Boswell's implication that Johnson "had no competitors" reflect a certain anxiety on their part regarding their readers' judgment of Johnson's central work. We see Hawkins and Boswell involved in a contradictory effort to influence this reception. They desire that *The Rambler* be compared to Addison and Steele's great works, not to the host of imitators (hence "he had no competitors"), but they also desire that Johnson's work not be compared to Addison and Steele's works as a redundant and derivative follower (hence "his way was open, and he had the choice of many paths").

The assumption that Johnson, in immediate competition with *The Tatler revived*, was himself attempting and not quite achieving "The Spectator revived" (which many might have thought a better title) is not confined to the eighteenth century. The modern judgment at its most generous is perhaps summarized by James Clifford: "If Johnson cannot quite ever catch the light touch of Addison and Steele, he does at times come close" (84). In his introduction to the Yale edition, W. Jackson Bate continues the strategy of encouraging us to distance the *Rambler* from the *Spectator* and its tradition by declaring that legacy only marginally significant: "If we concentrate merely on the periodical essay as it descended from Addison and Steele, or even if we confine ourselves too parochially to the eighteenth century itself," Bate warns, then "the true literary ancestry of the *Rambler* is overlooked, and our conception of it trivialized" (3:xxvii). But Bate has also shown us, in *The Burden of the Past and the English Poet*, how writers in the eighteenth century, reaching a crisis about 1750, were increasingly troubled by the problem of following earlier, definitive achievements. Surely any informed essayist of Johnson's era must recognize the inevitable comparison of his own work to *The Tatler*, *The Guardian*, and *The Spectator*, as the indirections of Boswell and Hawkins only begin to show. *The Tatler revived* obviously tries to turn this burden to its advantage. How does the other series launched in mid-March of 1750 deal with its inheritance? Is Johnson's work influenced by his awareness of his readers' assumption that anyone attempting a periodical essay is in some sense attempting to revive either *The Tatler* or *The Spectator*? Is he very much concerned with the problem of finding a voice after Addison and Steele have apparently said everything so well? Does Johnson manifest the same sort of contradictory impulses that motivate Hawkins and Boswell (and Bate in a different way) both to link and to distance Johnson with/from his famous predecessors?

Yes: Johnson is indeed so concerned that Harold Bloom's version of the more competitive and disruptive anxiety of influence seems better suited to Johnson's endeavor than Bate's more accommodating and inclusive burden of the past.[1] Bloom's well-known description of how strong writers make their own work possible by misreading their precursors is especially suggestive for Johnson, a strong writer to be sure, who repeatedly invokes and denies, incorporates and criticizes, imitates and departs from his most threatening and enabling forerunner, *The Spectator*. This antithetical revisionary stance can usefully be termed "deconstructive" only in the limited sense that Bloom is deconstructive. Although he explicitly rejects poststructuralism out of hand, in much the same way that Johnson rejects Berkeley (out of foot), Bloom has nonetheless often been linked to deconstruction, contributing to the landmark 1979 *Deconstruction and Criticism* along with Geoffrey Hartman, J. Hillis Miller, Paul de Man, and Jacques Derrida. Bloom shares

25

with these critics several assumptions regarding the creativity of criticism, the intertextuality of meaning, and the indeterminacy of texts, but his distinction, and his value here, lies in the particular way he uses the idea of our inevitable misreading to illuminate the relationships between "strong" writers and their texts. In fact, "there are no texts," Bloom declares with characteristic verve, "but only relationships between texts" (*Map* 3). For the strong writer such a relationship results from "an act of creative correction that is actually and necessarily a misinterpretation," as the later writer rebels against the earlier writer whom he also must emulate (*Anxiety* 30). Bloom's version of "deconstruction" is thus derived not from Saussure and linguistics but from Freud. Bloom's frame thus encourages us to look at *The Rambler* in terms of an Oedipal struggle with some powerful precursor whom Johnson must misread and displace to create a space for himself.[2]

Hawkins tells us that even at Oxford Johnson had a "great emulation, to call it by no worse a name, to excel his competitors in literature" (12). He never lost this passion to overcome others, even in "friendly" conversation, and he naturally tended to judge and rank whatever he observed. The passage taken as the epigraph to this chapter is revealing. According to William Maxwell's recollection,[3] Johnson asserted that the "noblest exhortation" by any heathen occurs in Homer, "the prince of poets," and concerns a patriarch's advice to surpass all mankind—which would obviously include overgoing the father himself. In this remark we see the results of a competition (conducted by Johnson) for the "noblest exhortation" in the special category of "heathen," as well as the unsurprising triumph of Homer in the ranking of poets. We further see Johnson celebrating a passage that presents life in competitive terms and advocates an extraordinary (verging on doomed) ambition with obvious Freudian implications. After applauding this exhortation "to outstrip always all mankind" (in Cowper's translation), Johnson observes, according to Maxwell, that "it was a most mortifying reflexion for any man to consider, *what he had done*, compared with what *he might have done*" (the emphasis is Maxwell's; Boswell 2:129).

Johnson early on found within himself an enormous drive to excel his competitors, even his literary fathers, as well as the heavy awareness that he had the extraordinary gifts to achieve such excellence. It was hardly sufficient that he, the son of a relatively unsuccessful bookseller, should succeed financially as a producer of books. As Boswell says, "From his earliest years, his superiority was perceived and acknowledged" (1:47). But this drive and awareness exacted a price. For instance, Johnson confided to Thomas Warton in 1754 that he "could not bear" the "superiority" of a particular Oxford classmate "at the classical lecture," and so he "tried to sit as far from him" as possible, so that he "might not hear him construe." Johnson shared this recollection, we may note, only after he and Wharton had visited the classmate, John Meeke, and Johnson had observed that "I used to think Meeke had excellent parts, . . . but, alas! 'Lost in a convent's solitary gloom!'" (Boswell 1:272). Are we thus surprised to find that the topic of envy, by Bate's count (*Achievement* 104), appears in some fifty-seven *Ramblers*, more than a quarter of the total? Or that Johnson, given such a goal of preeminence, always seemed to feel he should have done more, no matter what literary heights he scaled?[4]

In pursuing the representation of *The Spectator* in Johnson's series we will, as Bate warns, be narrowing our sense of *The Rambler*'s ancestry. My point is that we need to understand the extent to which Johnson involves us in precisely this fixation. "Montaigne and Bacon," Bate asserts in the introduction to the Yale Edition, "are the progenitors of the more straightforward moral essays in the *Rambler*" (3:xxvii). But Montaigne and Bacon and all other progenitors, whatever their influence, actually play a negligible role in Johnson's drama compared to Addison and Steele. The task of this chapter is to consider how Johnson writes within, against, over, and beyond *The Spectator*. Johnson's continuing concern with dead precursors "more outrageously alive than himself," as Bloom says (*Map* 19), is more than a psychological effect, biographically interesting. Rather, Johnson uses *The Spectator*—his creative misreading of it, that is—to help define his own series and position his audience. For Johnson as for Bloom, rhetoric includes the art of defense, quite literally (authorially speaking, anyway) a defense against the loss of self. But Johnson's strategies are not entirely the sort Bloom imagines. Johnson constitutes and maintains the voice of "the Rambler" in part by misreading *The Spectator*, and this focusing and dispersal serves an important persuasive function as Johnson inhabits *The Spectator*'s venerable tradition and also establishes the unique priority of his own series and its goals.

Because Johnson's sense of belatedness is at work from the very outset of his series, I try to examine with some care how *The Rambler* begins. I aim to dispel notions that Johnson's opening "has an improvisatory air," as Raman Selden says (270), or that Johnson "was not exactly sure what he meant to do," as Clifford says (77). By reading the opening essays closely, in sequence, and in light of *The Spectator*, we will get a better sense of the purposefulness and intelligence of Johnson's engagement with his most significant precursor, which will then be further substantiated by a broader consideration of the series as a whole. One particularly important aspect of Johnson's difference from Addison and Steele has to do with the character of Mr. Rambler as both imitation and antithesis of Mr. Spectator. This function will be addressed in a way that draws our attention to the role of another prominent feature of *The Spectator* (being misread) within *The Rambler*, the instruction and depiction of women.

"Forms of Salutation"

Whatever deconstruction's indiscretions (and the charges have been considerable), we have at least been sensitized to what is missing or marginal in a text. What is missing from *The Rambler*? According to Robert Olson, "There are no perceptible allusions to Addison and Steele or other English predecessors or contemporaries" in the first *Rambler* (1–2). Whether Olson is in fact correct depends upon how one defines "perceptible allusions," but his observation is in any case revealing. Olson, like any informed reader of this first essay, naturally expects that Johnson might well refer to Addison and Steele and situate his work within the periodical tradition. Johnson, eager to speak on his own of course,

finds himself in a tricky situation comparable to Boswell's and
Hawkins's dilemma just considered. If he refers directly to Addison
and Steele his reader's attention is deflected from his own work,
immediately establishing his secondary, derivative status. Yet if he
ignores his precursor entirely then his readers, as Olson proves,
also think of Addison and Steele, noticing their absence as much
or more than their presence. I argue that the opening essay reflects
a startling and perhaps impossible struggle, ingeniously conducted
and rhetorically effective, to deny the significance of a singularly
influential entity that Johnson does not want to name (wants in fact
to un-name) yet cannot ignore.

In Bloom's theory of literary creation, the writer's "individua-
tion" is made possible by an "initial love for the precursor's poetry"
that is "transformed rapidly enough into a revisionary strife" (*Map*
10). Johnson's desire to emulate or re-create *The Spectator*, his initial
love for the precursor, is manifested most immediately in the gross
anatomy of the series. We find numbered essays, all entitled by
the spokesman's metonymic name; epigraphs from authoritative
sources; correspondents; dream visions; literary criticism; short fiction; character studies; allegories; and deliberative essays—all part
of *The Spectator*'s format. Yet Johnson's sense of lateness and "revisionary strife" is already evident in the motto he chooses from
Juvenal for the first essay:

> Cur tamen hoc libeat potius decurrere campo,
> Per quem magnus equos Auruncae flexit alumnus
> Si vacat, et placidi rationem admittitis, edam.   (3:3)

Here is Elphinston's translation, which was added to the first bound
edition:

> Why to expatiate in this beaten field,
> Why arms, oft us'd in vain, I mean to wield;
> If time permit, and candour will attend,
> Some satisfaction this essay may lend.

The reference to "arms, oft us'd in vain" and a "beaten field"
certainly seems to reflect Johnson's awareness of his tardy appear-

29

ance, entering a tradition already fatigued with combatants. But Juvenal's text, which appeared without translation in the original issue, focuses on a single precursor, promising to explain why "it should please me to run through the same field in which the great horses of the offspring of Aurunca were turned."[5] Lucilius, the "offspring of Aurunca" (his birthplace), established the satiric tradition Juvenal attempts to join. Who can fill this role for Johnson other than Addison and Steele, fathers of the tradition he is attempting to enter?

Johnson's invocation here—using Juvenal's voice, silent himself—is clear enough: Lucilius is to Juvenal as Addison and Steele are to Johnson. This once-removed admission that he follows after *The Spectator* is further muted by adding Elphinston's translation, which shifts our attention to the open field and available arms. Johnson's undertaking, secondary with respect to his Lucilius, becomes a fresh start with respect to his other failed competitors. Johnson displaces his expected allusion to *The Spectator* (using Juvenal) then later suppresses it (using Elphinston).

The notion that Mr. Rambler is going to run over the same field as Mr. Spectator is arguably already suggested by Johnson's title. The similarities are evident. The Spectator stands apart, uninvolved, watching life go by; obversely, the Rambler moves through life watching, also unattached. Mr. Spectator, we quickly learn, derives his "exact Neutrality" from his status as "a Spectator of Mankind" rather than "one of the Species" (1:4). Mr. Rambler likewise declares himself "a kind of neutral being" able to consider human problems "in the cool maturity of life" without becoming entangled in them (3:98). Mr. Spectator reveals in the opening paper that he is a grave and silent man with "an insatiable thirst after Knowledge," having applied "so much Diligence to my Studies that there are few celebrated Books, either in the Learned or the Modern Tongues, which I am not acquainted with." Mr. Rambler discloses that he has "long studied the severest and most abstracted philosophy"—which almost makes Mr. Spectator's claim to be acquainted with most of the "celebrated" books seem shallow.

Given Addison and Steele's enormous popularity, many of Johnson's readers may well have recalled that Mr. Spectator refers at the beginning of his third issue to one of his recent "Rambles, or Speculations." For Johnson to have lifted his title from this passage would not have been remarkable. One of the century's last *Spectator* offspring, William Roberts's *The Looker-On*, which began in 1792, obviously takes its title from Mr. Spectator's characterization of himself in Addison and Steele's first issue as a "Looker-on" (1:5). And Mr. Looker-On also enjoys a "rigid neutrality" after his "great many years in the pursuits of literature and philosophy," as he says in his first issue. He indeed removes himself so far from life's disturbances that he even abstains from eating peppers or "any thing that can raise the smallest combustion" (1:13).

Despite such shared conventions (neutrality, detachment, scholarship, shifting vision), Mr. Rambler and Mr. Spectator and the periodicals they inhabit are presented quite differently. Addison begins the first *Spectator* with the observation that "a Reader seldom peruses a Book with pleasure" without some detailed knowledge of its author (1:1), and Johnson's reader might naturally expect that the first *Rambler*, like the initial *Spectator*, would offer a sketch of the spokesman, covering his birth, childhood, education, character, and habits. For Steele's *Guardian* this conventional introduction is motivated as much by the writer's desire to display himself as by the reader's desire to know, for "there is no passion so universal . . . as the passion of being known to the rest of mankind," not only in "parts, virtues, or qualifications," but even in "physiognomy" (7). But however essayists might justify this introduction, Mr. Spectator's "astonishingly vivid" initial portrait of himself, as the standard edition's editor terms it (1:1n.2), was easily the model of how to begin an essay series. Part of this portrait's appeal, no doubt, is Mr. Spectator's bouyant confidence as he promises to share his "many useful Discoveries" "for the Benefit of my Contemporaries" (1:5) and "the Advancement of the Publick Weal" (1:6). Although he retains some comic mystery, keeping his name, age, lodgings, complexion, and dress "very great Secrets," even these, he says, may be disclosed later. Mr. Spectator's shyness in person, his "most profound silence" (1:2), is thus ironically opposed to his willingness "to print my self out" so openly (1:5).

So how does Johnson get started? He writes as if *The Spectator* did not exist, as if he were attempting to invent the periodical essay, beginning by considering the problem of how to begin—"The difficulty of the first address on any new occasion" (3:3). Although Johnson recognizes that there are "settled and regular forms of salutation" in "all languages," these have no intrinsic or natural rightness, having been imposed arbitrarily by "necessity." This point is illustrated by a compressed allegory in which "Judgment was wearied with the perplexity of being forced upon choice, where there was no motive to preference." The story of these first two sentences of *The Rambler*, involving the self-conscious analysis of the undecidability of questions grounded in linguistic convention, leading to arbitrary choice, will be played out repeatedly in greater detail in the rest of this initial essay and throughout the series. It is a narrative that epitomizes Johnson's central theory of how one might move beyond uncertainty, even the radical sort we call deconstruction, into the realm of choice, action, and faith.

Johnson first addresses the problem of beginning in the most expansive sense, progressing to the question of how to begin an essay series. Any writer, Johnson observes, naturally wishes for "such ceremonial modes of entrance" as the various languages have adopted for greetings. In the case of heroic poetry, we all know that the Homeric formula has been embraced. Unfortunately, "hitherto," Johnson says, invoking a judicial rigor, a settled form for beginning "has never been legally extended to the lower orders of literature" (3:4). If writers have adopted a conventional beginning in genres like the essay series, they have acted without warrant, assuming a law that does not exist. Should a settled form now be extended to the essay series? How, "legally," might such a convention be established?

Johnson does not say, for to consider such issues would raise one obvious solution to the problem of beginning: follow *The Spectator*, introducing the spokesman and arousing our interest and expectation. So Johnson turns away from this problem, avoiding *The Spectator*'s beginning, which would then take over *The Rambler*'s beginning. He refers instead to Horace's assertion that "it is more pleasing to see smoke brightening into flame, than flame sinking into smoke," thus providing a blanket injunction against imita-

32

[handwritten marginal note:] one must first assume
it is a problem for J.[?] [?]
one must beg the question.

tion—consistent with his pronouncement 153 essays later that "no man ever yet became great by imitation." The implication is clear. By invoking a great predecessor, the writer may sabotage his own project, raising expectations he may be unable to meet, ensuring a demanding judgment.

Although Johnson suppresses Addison and Steele's beginning in one sense, he returns to it in another, for this precept of Horace, deployed against imitation, is the beginning of *The Spectator*, its opening motto to be precise. In quoting Horace's claim (which Johnson has revised), "Not smoke after flame does he plan to give, but after smoke the light, that then he may set forth striking and wondrous tales," Addison certainly attempts to raise expectations—the strategy Johnson declines. While Horace's precept in the context of the first *Spectator* is simply a scholarly way of claiming the series will be excellent, within Johnson's revisionary essay the quote implies that Addison, beginning with a blaze of expectations, is quoting a precept that contradicts his own practice. Johnson thus not only justifies his own departure from Addison and Steele but also strikingly manages, if we should return to their beginning, to impugn it.

Johnson goes on to acknowledge that, despite "the authority of Horace" and "the general opinion of the world," some writers (Addison and Steele might have been mentioned, but remain unnamed) have praised their own works, perhaps because they "imagined themselves entitled by indisputable merit to an exemption from general restraints" (3:5). We may wonder why such self-promotion, which certainly sounds offensive, is not immediately rejected by Johnson—until we realize that the unknown author of *The Rambler* has somehow to get his own work recommended to the public. Thucydides, we are reminded, informed his audience of the value of his work, and "it may, indeed," Johnson admits, "be no less dangerous to claim, on certain occasions, too little than too much." So, should the essayist praise himself?

At this point Johnson reproduces in different terms his opening scene, in which "Judgment was wearied with the perplexity of being forced upon choice, where there was no motive to preference" (3:3). We find that Plutarch does not include "an author entering

33

the world" among those who may justly "proclaim his own excellencies" (so the answer is "no"), unless he fits into the category of those who cannot otherwise be recommended (so the answer may be "yes"). But an author unavoidably recommends himself in the very act of publishing (so the answer must be "no"). Yet such an implicit recommendation may not be carefully evaluated by fickle readers without a more explicit one (so is the answer yes or no?). If he praises himself, Johnson falls in with those conceited writers who imagined their indisputable merits. If he fails to recommend himself, then who will pay any attention? So Johnson in some sense waffles his way out of the dilemma. But at the same time he has implied that his appearance is itself an unarticulated self-recommendation and that his audience, unless they consider themselves fickle, should read him with care. It is a brilliant strategy.

Having expended eight paragraphs of openly unresolved analysis on the question of how to begin, Johnson now offers a more oblique approach. Perhaps writing can be compared to courtship, thus raising the possibility of "indirect and unperceived approaches" that might allow the seductive writer to "glide imperceptibly" into possession of the reader's favors. Enacting the strategy he is considering, Johnson goes on to hypothesize that since successful lovers strategically "conceal their passion," perhaps an author should "proclaim his pretensions to literary honours" only when he is "sure of not being rejected" (3:6). These options too seem to fall apart when we realize that "the world supposes every man that writes ambitious of applause, as some ladies have taught themselves to believe that every man intends love." (We are ourselves seeing this indirection in this critique of indirectness.) The author thus exists in a "hazardous state" because his readers, like sensible ladies, are naturally on guard. Whether one should proceed openly, deceptively, confessing weakness, or declaring greatness, is still unclear. But historically, Johnson finally acknowledges, the "diurnal writers"—again Addison and Steele, the exemplars of this class, will not be named—have usually opted for an "ostentatious and haughty display of themselves." This damaging observation is qualified in a way that also tends to trivialize such writers:

"If their boasts deceive any into the perusal of their performances, they defraud them of but little time" (3:6–7).

If the periodical writer cannot begin with a formula (none are recognized for an essay series), or the imitation of a predecessor (it raises damaging expectations), or an apology (it is disregarded), or a self-recommendation (it is offensive), or an indirect recommendation (it is impossible), then how can one begin other than by analyzing the obstructions to beginning?

Thus Johnson projects the sort of metalepsis or reversal that Bloom considers the most crucial defense of the ephebe against the precursor (*Anxiety* 16), making it appear impossible now for the earlier series properly to begin (to have begun), as if *The Spectator* were actually later, as if Johnson has returned to a more original moment prior to the periodical tradition, which he is now launching. At this moment in Johnson's anti-beginning, perplexed again by a choice with "no motive to preference," an "I" appears, announcing his intention "to endeavour the entertainment of my countrymen by a short essay on Tuesday and Saturday" (3:7). If he is not "commended for the beauty of my works," this emergent author hopes "to be at least pardoned for their brevity." This posture is so patently pitiful, so strikingly different from Addison and Steele's ambition, we must wonder whether to laugh or sympathize, in equipoise ourselves.

In other words, the problem of how to address his readers has not been solved, at least not explicitly, and is being abandoned in order to address them. One could argue, in fact, that the various options considered—submission, indirection, formula, imitation, boldness—have all been employed in the process of being rejected. In any event, Johnson, or Mr. Rambler, or the "I" who finally appears, announces he will not disclose "whether my expectations are most fixed on pardon or praise," for "having accurately weighed the reasons for arrogance and submission, I find them so nearly equiponderant, that my impatience to try the event of my first performance will not suffer me to attend any longer the trepidations of the balance" (3:7)—a statement that offers one more image of undecidability repudiated by choice, exposing Johnson to a critique of neither position, a critique dismantled by his will to act. Unable to decide how to begin, unwilling to disclose his stance, he is beginning.

In this action there is at least the consolation that brief, varied papers have "many conveniencies." Surely, we are told, "he that questions his abilities to arrange the dissimilar parts of an extensive plan, or fears to be lost in a complicated system, may yet hope to adjust a few pages without perplexity" (3:8). But the "I," who just announced his appearance, is already "lost," having slipped into the anonymity of the third person, as the essay writer in general is considered: "He" may "rectify his opinions" by "attending the remarks which every paper will produce," changing his topics to catch the "aura popularis," even abandoning "an unwieldy subject" (3:8).

As these advantages add up, they also implicitly raise questions about the difficulty of writing, even in the genre of essays. One may "hope," as Johnson says, to adjust a few pages without difficulty, but can one actually do it? Even if he could assimilate all the various "remarks which every paper will produce," would those comments allow for a coherent and constructive response, or would numerous and conflicting suggestions leave the writer even more confused? Such a beginning may naturally lead one to think of ending, and the initial *Rambler* does in fact conclude by observing that if the writer finds, "with all his industry, and all his artifices . . . he cannot deserve regard, or cannot attain it," then "he may let the design fall at once." This possibility of immediately ending at the outset starts to look even more attractive since "without injury to others or himself" the writer may "retire to amusements of greater pleasure, or to studies of better prospect" (3:8). Thus, this shadowy speaker, whom I am sometimes calling "Johnson" for the moment, concludes his "appearance" by pointing to his future absence, representing his ambition and his identity in the form of their negation or at least suspension (momentarily suspended). As Bloom repeatedly argues, the strong writer's work originates in a refusal of death.[6] Johnson's willingness to withdraw—at odds with the exacting analysis of how to appear—is both a manipulative and a defensive gesture towards such a refusal, eliciting the reader's approval so the Rambler doesn't do away with himself, yet also separating his identity from an authorial self who may cease to exist "without injury to . . . himself." Johnson wins his initial struggle with his dead precursors, outrageously alive, the same way the *Rambler* will advocate we defeat death: by looking beyond it to a greater good.

Whereas the second *Spectator* expands upon "the Club," introducing Sir Roger de Coverly, the Templar, Sir Andrew Freeport, Captain Sentry, Will Honeycomb, and the Clergyman, no club is created for the elusive Mr. Rambler, despite Johnson's own enthusiasms. Instead, the second *Rambler* further displays Johnson's defensive strategies of belatedness by focusing on another difficulty of writing, one most acutely felt by the writer appearing later: how to approach a topic that everyone knows how to handle, a topic so familiar that "a train of sentiments" automatically arises, rendering "authors willing rather to transmit than examine so advantageous a principle" (3:9–10). To drive home just how depleted the topic is, Johnson piles up his supporting statements beyond any apparent need, virtually exhausting the exhaustion of this topic, perhaps even proving the reader's natural restlessness by exacerbating it. The practice of "looking forward into futurity"

> has been ridiculed with all the pleasantry of wit, and exaggerated with all the amplifications of rhetoric. Every instance, by which its absurdity might appear most flagrant, has been studiously collected; it has been marked with every epithet of contempt, and all the tropes and figures have been called forth against it. (3:9)

So we now have an author who first cannot determine how to begin and threatens to quit, and who then starts to write, redundantly, on a topic that has been used up. In the first essay, he appears to lack any precedent he can invoke; in the second, he appears to be overwhelmed by precedents. While Mr. Spectator writes out of fullness and potency, promising "to print myself out," Mr. Rambler finds, so it seems, that the totality of wit, rhetoric, anecdote, satire, and style are already in print.

Johnson's strategy again involves undoing this prior and closed discussion, for this "common topic," dismissed in effect by being routinely transmitted, is determined to be in fact incorrect. It is actually fortunate that the mind is dissatified with the "objects immediately before it," constantly "losing itself in schemes of future felicity." Otherwise "there would," Johnson says, "be few enterprises of great labour or hazard undertaken, if we had not the power of magnifying the advantages which we persuade ourselves to expect from them" (3:11). Thus, in an authoritative reversal, Johnson returns us to the moment before this issue was decided. We must examine it afresh.

The "luxurious indulgence of hope," Johnson acknowledges, can of course be disastrous, and authors are especially subject to this excess. At just this point an "I" again appears, illustrating authorial desire by once more detaching himself from the reader's influence and alienating himself from his own ambition. "I shall, therefore, while I am yet but lightly touched with the symptoms of the writer's malady, endeavour to fortify myself against the infection" (3:12). Although "there is nothing more dreadful to an author than neglect," this "I," passing (as in the first essay) to third-person speculation, innoculates himself (again as in the first essay) with precisely that prospect, for "he that endeavours after fame by writing, solicits the regard of a multitude fluctuating in pleasures, or immersed in business," or "prepossessed by passions, or corrupted by prejudices" (3:14). Any author who succeeds, the essay concludes, "is indebted to other causes besides his industry, his learning, or his wit." Although there is little impetus here to read these "other causes" in religious terms, as the series progresses this compulsion will become stronger. In a sense, that is what the *Rambler* is about—exposing our vulnerabilites, confronting what we most fear, directing our attention beyond ourselves until we glimpse some "other causes" at work.

The promise in the first essay to "endeavour the entertainment of my countrymen" is carried out in an unexpected way in the initial two essays, and the third *Rambler* is equally surprising, as it begins by continuing the second issue's self-conscious complaint in virtually the same terms. The second essay's last paragraph and the third essay's first paragraph both analyze the writer's task in the same binary terms, noting the difficulty of either alternative approach to composing. Whether the author attempts to "teach what is not known" or to "recommend known truths," he faces a "very difficult" labor since the audience is naturally reluctant to "confess their ignorance" or "allow that he from whom they are to learn is more knowing than themselves" (3:15). The writer's competition thus extends beyond his precursors and contemporaries even to his readers. Johnson's strategy here involves undermining the reader's resistance by acknowledging and explaining it, and the allegory making up the rest of this issue likewise disarms adverse response by telling us how Criticism's duties have been turned over to Time, even though Flattery and Malevolence now roam the earth pretending to make Criticism's determinations.

Thus, the third *Rambler*, like the third *Spectator*, features an allegory. But Addison's story of Publick Credit's demise and miraculous revival seems unrelated to the two preceding essays. In fact, it conflicts with the opening issue's promise of political neutrality. Although Johnson's essays thus far are not explicitly linked to each other (or *The Spectator*), they are focused on the same topic, writing and its reception, and, moreover, work toward essentially the same effect—at once precluding while articulating the reader's resistance and containing while exposing the author's ambition. No readers will want to include themselves in the "virulent generation" of *Rambler* 3, or the pea-brained, restive "multitude" of *Rambler* 2, or the fickle, suspicious "world" of *Rambler* 1. Having considered the difficulties of writing, what reader can resist some sympathy and generosity toward a well-intentioned author, especially one who acknowledges and struggles against his own desire, positing other pursuits of "greater pleasure" or "better prospect"?

Johnson's fourth essay, startlingly enough, after having shown the virtual impossibility of criticism in the preceding essay, is (what else?) an act of criticism. In this famous consideration of moral fiction, assumed to be a comparison of Fielding and Richardson, Johnson continues his construction of the reader's response by focusing on the proper grounds for evaluating writing. Quite simply, according to Johnson we must recognize that in the larger scheme of things "virtue is the highest proof of understanding, and the only solid basis of greatness" (3:25). The fourth *Spectator* appears to address a similar topic, the behavior of an author and his audience. Mr. Spectator reveals the ineptitude of some readers and, like Mr. Rambler, detaches himself from their regard, vowing to be "very careful of the Design of my Actions, but very negligent of the Consequences of them," given the obtuseness and caprice of readers (1:18). The fourth *Rambler*, however, without mentioning the fourth *Spectator*, serves as a pointed response to its position, for Johnson's thesis is that the author is certainly responsible for the consequences of his work. It is, in fact, precisely those less capable readers whose response most deserves our attention—"the young, the ignorant, and the idle," who have "minds unfurnished with ideas, and therefore susceptible of impressions" (3:21).

Mr. Rambler thus exhibits himself working to shift even his own attention from himself to the reader, defending himself against failure by displacing (once again) himself. The author is not so important that he cannot always quit (*Rambler* 1); he should remember that merit does not guarantee success (*Rambler* 2), largely because today's Critics follow Flattery and Malevolence (*Rambler* 3); the effect of the author upon the reader, and not vice-versa, is of the utmost importance (*Rambler* 4). Mr. Spectator, on the other hand, keeps the spotlight on himself. Steele's *Spectator* 4 is really devoted to drawing more sharply Mr. Spectator's character by detailing his determined silence and obscurity. Despite his declared disregard for his reception, Mr. Spectator concludes this essay by asserting that "the greatest Glory of my Work" will be its use "among reasonable Women" to "furnish *Tea-Table Talk*" (1:21). This ambition, innocent and even amusing within *The Spectator*, seems quite myopic from the vantage point of the *The Rambler* and its opening assault on the writer's glory, and the idea of appealing especially to women will later be attacked by Johnson more substantially.

Thus, as Addison and Steele proceed, Mr. Spectator continues to emerge as a delightful and memorable character within an appreciative community. True to his name, Mr. Spectator reports on his observation of others, but his immediate interest, and in a sense the reader's, continues to be his own personality. As he says, "The working of my own Mind, is the general Entertainment of my Life" (1:21). Mr. Rambler, on the other hand, follows this opening sequence of essays on writing with a clustering devoted to "the moral discipline of the mind, and . . . the increase of virtue rather than of learning," which is declared in the eighth essay to be the purpose of the entire series (3:42). Mr. Rambler, in other words, pressing on his isolation, tries to ignore himself, with qualified success. Addison and Steele without a doubt were not uninterested in the increase of virtue, but Johnson's opening sequence seems designed to trivialize his predecessor, suggesting a dramatic difference of strategy, as *The Rambler* closely follows *The Spectator* while explicitly ignoring it in a way that reveals why the second should come first.

"In a State of Unavoidable Comparison"

Johnson's effort to write over *The Spectator*—in Bloom's terms, the crucial "misprision" or misreading of his predecessors—is not merely an opening or incidental or deeply hidden gesture. In fact, one of the most interesting things about the unfavorable comparisons of *The Rambler* to *The Spectator* is the way such judgments are modelled within *The Rambler* itself, as Mr. Rambler's suppression and distortion of his predecessor gives way to a defense of himself against the advice, critiques, and attacks of Addison and Steele's loyal fans—who are mostly Johnson's creation! Some sense of the pervasiveness of this imitation/rejection relationship will help to clarify two of its most interesting features, the character of "Mr. Rambler" and the depiction of women.

A thoroughly typical response is presented in number 97 by Samuel Richardson, one of Johnson's few real-life correspondents, who is given the forum of *The Rambler* in order to criticize it. Richardson, introduced as "an author from whom the age has received greater favors" (4:97), recalls the "pleasure" and "amusements" of *The Spectator*, and he wishes Mr. Rambler would "oftener take cognizance of the manners of the better half of the human species," so that "if your precepts and observations be carried down to posterity, the *Spectators* may shew to the rising generation what were the fashionable follies of their grandmothers, the *Rambler* of their mothers, and that from both they may draw instruction and warning" (4:154).

Richardson, who read the series irregularly, may not have realized how unoriginal a suggestion he was making.[7] The tenth *Rambler* had already featured a particularly interesting collection of criticisms, especially when it is read against the tenth *Spectator*, in many respects its mirror image. Both spokesmen at that point take time out to assess their reception thus far. Addison has Mr. Spectator start by tallying up "with much satisfaction" the number of his "disciples" in London and Westminster: three thousand papers times twenty readers per paper—a "modest Computation," he says—equals an incredible sixty thousand readers. Mr. Rambler similarly refers in the first sentence of his tenth issue to "the number of correspondents which encreases every day upon me," a hopeful if less specific accounting than Addison's, as we assume the growth in correspondents indicates an increasing popularity. But his second sentence moves to invert the implications of the first, as Mr. Rambler says "It is no less a proof of eminence to have many enemies than many friends."[8]

In addition to this stark contrast, with one series apparently gathering "enemies" and the other "disciples," Mr. Spectator promises his readership "faithfully" to stop writing "as soon as I grow dull," while Johnson's spokesman at this point twice declares himself to be completely unaffected by his audience's negative reaction, with one exception. "The only pain, which I can feel from my correspondence," Mr. Rambler says, "is the fear of disgusting those, whose letters I shall neglect." But he eases his heart of this "only apprehension that sat heavy upon it" by reminding his rejected or neglected correspondents that "I only return the treatment, which I often receive"; and that his motives may be "known only to himself"; and that "not all letters . . . postponed are rejected, nor all that are rejected, critically condemned." This response makes, I think, a real contribution to the genre of rejection letters, profoundly muddling the reasons why any particular submission may have been overlooked, and how Mr. Rambler really feels about it. The suspicion that Mr. Rambler has simply "dispatched" his correspondents, as he puts it later in the essay, is reinforced by the Virgilian motto for this essay, "Posthabui tamen illorum mea seria ludo," which Johnson translates as "For trifling sports I quitted grave affairs." The motto for the tenth *Spectator*, also taken from Virgil, similarly speaks of taking a break from one's labour: "As if one, whose oars can scarce force his skiff against the stream, should by chance slacken his arms, and lo! headlong down the current the channel sweeps it away."[9] Whereas Addison finds that slackening miraculously propels him toward his goal, Johnson presents exactly the opposite situation, in which the necessity for lightening up impedes his work. Again, as in the opening sequence, we see that Mr. Rambler struggles to insulate himself from his readers, even though he cannot abandon his desire for "eminence" (and must satisfy it by counting enemies). As a result he announces that he derives his value not from such "trifling sports" but from more serious affairs, presumably the moral purpose announced in *Rambler* 8.

Mr. Spectator in his tenth essay describes four kinds of audiences sure to be interested in the series, while Mr. Rambler quotes four particular respondents who are for various reasons disappointed. By including these four "helpful" letters, which were all apparently written by Hester Mulso, Johnson shapes our perception of the desire for *The Rambler* to be more like *The Spectator*. Most obviously, the allusive struggle with his precursor is now brought into the open by these correspondents. First, "a set of candid readers" wishes that he would "now and then throw in, like his predecessor, some papers of a gay and humorous turn." Then "a lady" informs Mr. Rambler that "if he is a mere essayist, and troubles not himself with the manners of the age, she is sorry to tell him, that even the genius and correctness of an Addison will not secure him from neglect." Next "Lady Racket" invites him to cards because "she hopes to see his papers interspersed with living characters," like the earlier series, one assumes. Finally "a modest young man" offers "to assist" Mr. Rambler—to become, it seems, the Steele to Johnson's Addison. Thus, all four of these well-intentioned suggestions—to "throw in" "living characters," "the manners of the age," "gay and humorous" papers, and a coauthor—are advising Mr. Rambler to imitate more closely "his predecessor."

This advice, following Johnson's restatement of his purpose as "the moral discipline of the mind," revising his opening promise to entertain his countrymen, emphasizes the differences (as Johnson is presenting them) between the two projects. In the tenth *Spectator* Addison had promised to furnish conversational topics for "the Blanks of Society," who have no ideas; to instruct and delight those "well regulated families" who will serve his paper with their tea; to assist his "Fraternity of Spectators," who desire "to form a right Judgment of those who are the Actors" on the world's stage; and to "divert the Minds of my female Readers from greater Trifles" while also pointing out "the Blemishes" and the virtues of "the Sex" (1:44–47). Mr. Rambler's correspondents desire this sort of light entertainment and authoritative direction, which seems worthy enough in *The Spectator*. Johnson's idea of "entertainment" is more serious, and while the moral discipline of the mind may not be as much fun as lesser trifles, Johnson is claiming and implicitly urging his readers toward the higher ground. In such a context, Johnson's correspondents make the earlier series seem trivial.

Not surprisingly, we see no evidence that Mr. Rambler will heed the correspondents' advice, and he certainly will not appease Flirtilla by celebrating masquerades. As Bloom argues, however, the ephebe's relationship to his precursor, who is both "a liberating angel and blocking-agent, perpetual irritant and solacing glory" (*Ringers* 269), is inherently ambivalent. Mr. Rambler does allow "a man of high reputation in gay life" to vindicate that glorious entertainment "where all the outworks of chastity are at once demolished"—just the sort of ironical humor Addison and Steele purveyed. He is thus able to refuse and include imitations of his predecessor.

In responding to these billets, Mr. Rambler actually refers to "one of my predecessors," and his plural (in *Rambler* 23 Mr. Rambler will again refer to plural "predecessors"), in contradistinction to

the correspondent's singular "predecessor" (in *Rambler* 126 another
correspondent will also use the singular), is itself a subtle denial of
the *Spectator*'s dominating presence, even as the source of his remark reinforces it. He refuses to acknowledge a singular forerunner, yet the authority he quotes in support is Steele—from *Spectator*
484. Throughout the series, in fact, the incorporation of the *Spectator*
into the *Rambler* is marked by the same sort of call for what is
missing, the dismissal of what is there, and the inclusion of what
is supposedly denied.

For example, Mr. Rambler opens up a perfect topic for Addison and Steele when he reports in *Rambler* 15 that "there is no
grievance, public, or private, of which, since I took upon me the
office of a periodical monitor, I have received so many, or so earnest
complaints, as of the predominance of play" (3:80). *Spectator* 140 in
fact includes a letter ridiculing those women who gamble, trans-
forming themselves from gentle souls into "the veriest Wasps"
(2:54). Mr. Rambler, however, responds to these complaints by
saying, "I have found, by long experience, that there are few enterprises so hopeless as contests with the fashion," thus emphasizing
his lack of interest in the "fashionable follies" so engrossing to his
precursor and its many followers. Although Mr. Rambler will not
contest with fashion, Johnson actually fabricates two letters from
"readers" who show how gambling makes *men* into fools (rejecting
the misogynous direction of his correspondent).

Rambler 34 is another instance of such a double move. Mr.
Rambler reports that "I have been censured for having hitherto
dedicated so few of my speculations to the ladies" (3:184), and he
responds with a double-edged admission and counteraccusation:
"Indeed the moralist, whose instructions are accommodated to only
one half of the human species, must be confessed not sufficiently
to have extended his views." He acknowledges that "the peculiar
virtues or faults of women" may have played "too small" a part
in "philosophical discourses" given the enormous happiness and
influence in their hands. Even so, "masculine duties afford more
room for counsels and observations, as they are less uniform, and
connected with things more subject to vicissitudes and accident"
(3:184). If he has erred in one direction, the implication is clear

enough that his predecessors, who dedicated so many of their speculations to the ladies, erred in the other. Avoiding the issue himself, Johnson, or Mr. Rambler, prints a letter "which perhaps may not be wholly useless to them whose chief ambition is to please." This endorsement is shrewdly feeble. Any woman intelligent enough to be reading *The Rambler* may well have a higher ambition than merely "to please," and there is a certain lack of enthusiasm in the phrase "may not be wholly useless." Thus Johnson is able to present a satiric view of feminine delicacy in the story of Anthea, inhabiting the *Spectator*'s tradition, while distancing such limited, sportive writing from Mr. Rambler and his "grave affairs," asserting his revisionary status.

It is helpful to consider how this sort of complementarity tends to create the sense of two *Ramblers*, one written by Mr. Rambler, which offers serious and perhaps even sour pronouncements instead of "humour and the manners of the world," and the other written by the correspondents, who complain about Mr. Rambler and even attempt to provide what he does not. This duality helps to create conflict and drama, allowing Johnson to do contrary things, appeasing those who have gotten an inflexible idea of an essay series from his predecessor, and at the same time also offering a more serious and substantial alternative. This technique, dividing his own series while separating it from the earlier one, is of course prefigured by Mr. Spectator's interaction with his correspondents, linking Mr. Rambler to his predecessor as he strives to distinguish himself. Such a relationship is identified by Bloom as a common strategy deployed by the strong writer against his forerunner, and Bloom compares this phenomenon to Freud's concept of *Verneinung*, or negation, by which a repressed idea is both articulated and disowned (see *Poetry* 18–34).

Even the literary criticism in the series contributes to this continuation and negation of *The Spectator* in *The Rambler*. The most sustained critical effort in Johnson's series focuses on Milton, a "dangerous" choice as *Rambler* 86 says, because it places Johnson's work "in a state of unavoidable comparison with excellence"— a choice made even more dangerous because the "excellence is consecrated by death" (4:87). Johnson is not talking in fact about

Milton, but rather about Milton's most famous critic. If Addison cannot be blamed for being dead or excellent, the writer who follows after his eighteen celebrated essays on Milton nonetheless faces an unfair situation. "He stands under the shade of exalted merit, and is hindered from rising to his natural height, by the interception of those beams which should invigorate and quicken him" (4:87); "The imitator treads a beaten walk, and with all his diligence can only hope to find a few flowers or branches untouched by his predecessor, the refuse of contempt, or the omissions of negligence" (4:88).

In employing such a strained horticultural drama—the young tree stunted and choked and the almost barren walk, depicting first an overgrown then a defoliated landscape—Johnson is already setting Addison up. By so thoroughly depreciating himself—hoping that "however I may fall below the illustrious writer who has so long dictated to the commonwealth of learning, my attempt may not be wholly useless"—Johnson will use the lowly vehicle of versification to expose the missing foundation of Addison's critical mausoleum. Addison has overlooked versification, Johnson says, "not probably because he thought the art of numbers unworthy of his notice" (4:88), for surely Addison "knew with how minute attention the ancient criticks considered the dispositions of syllables." (At least, we would have assumed he knew until Johnson raised the issue.) Addison, "being the first," obviously "had many objects at once before him" and therefore seems to have "passed willingly over those" that "required labour, rather than genius" (4:88–89). Avoiding labor, ignoring the precedent of the ancients, Addison has been praised to the point that his priority now seems merely temporal, a simple matter of "being the first," putting the unavoidably later at a disadvantage, obstructing his opportunity to thrive and bloom.

In fact, Johnson proceeds to show how Addison despite his advantage has really overlooked the most fundamental concern, for versification is not only "indispensably necessary to a poet," it is even what gives poetry its "peculiar superiority," distinguishing poetry from prose. Johnson, arriving late on the scene, after Addison has harvested whatever he wishes, finds his predecessor has ignored the primary, quintessential concern—and thus again inserts himself beforehand, momentarily silencing his dead precursor who appeared to have been already saying just about everything.

Similarly, in *Rambler* 158, Johnson observes how "it is established at present, that the proemial lines of a poem . . . must be void of glitter and embellishment," a precept traced to Addison's observation that "the first lines of *Paradise Lost* are perhaps as plain, simple, and unadorned as any of the whole poem, in which particular the author has conformed himself to the example of Homer and the precept of Horace" (5:78). Addison has apparently adopted "the common opinion" here, Johnson says, for he certainly has not consulted "the precept or example." Horace mentions only content, not expression; and Homer's "exordial verses" are "eminently adorned and illuminated" (5:79). Johnson proposes instead of Addison's observation, which turns out to be incorrect in both attribution and content, a more commonsensical precept—one that reflects, I would say, on his own beginning: "The intent of the introduction is to raise expectation, and suspend it; something therefore must be discovered, and something concealed; and the poet, while the fertility of his invention is yet unknown, may properly recommend himself by the grace of his language" (5:80).

Again, in *Rambler* 93 Johnson refutes Addison's assertion that "a true critick" "points out beauties rather than faults" (4:134). Earlier in this essay Johnson has already noted how Addison "is suspected to have denied the expediency of poetical justice, because his own *Cato* was condemned to perish in a good cause" (4:132), thus damaging Addison's credibility. With regard to observing faults—about which an author/critic can hardly be objective—Johnson first undermines Addison's point by observing that for critics of genius "it is rather natural" to study writers with "more beauties than faults" (4:134). Addison's observation is therefore not that useful. But Johnson goes further: "The duty of criticism is neither to depreciate, nor dignify by partial representations, but to hold out the light of reason, whatever it may discover." In the case of celebrated writers, Johnson says, ignoring faults is "more dangerous" because their influence is "more extensive." If their shortcomings are not "discovered and stigmatized," these errors will "have the sanction of antiquity conferred upon them, and become precedents of indisputable authority" (4:134).

Coming in the midst of his critical series on Milton, this conclusion implicitly defends Johnson's preceding discovery in *Rambler* 88 that Milton "seems to have somewhat mistaken the nature of our language" and as a result has produced passages in which "the music is injured" and "the meaning is obscured" (4:102, 103). The conclusion that errors should be exposed also supports Johnson's subsequent finding in *Rambler* 94 that in relating sound to sense Milton has "certainly committed a fault like that of the player, who looked on the earth when he implored the heavens, and to the heavens when he addressed the earth" (4:141–42). On the positive side, Johnson finds in *Rambler* 90 that in his handling of pauses and gaps between lines, Milton "has performed all that our language would admit" (4:115)—an interesting compliment to say the least, as Milton is admitted to have handled very well that part of the language where (in a sense) there isn't any. Thus Johnson is able to question the "indisputable authority" of both Milton and his critic, undermining on two fronts the priority of the earlier writer.

"A Kind of Neutral Being"

The idea that Johnson constructs a drama in which Mr. Rambler tends in various ways to oppose *The Spectator*, while his correspondents in some sense tend to continue it, requires us to look more closely at Mr. Rambler. Thus far I have been speaking somewhat indiscriminately of "Johnson" and "Mr. Rambler." Is Mr. Rambler a mask for Johnson, or a character in Johnson's drama? How is Mr. Rambler therefore different from Mr. Spectator? According to Howard Weinbrot's penetrating study of Pope and his masks, "the eighteenth century inherited and used a complex, though not universally accepted, theory of the persona," a theory that recognized "the persona as a mask portraying an idealized . . . speaker" but that also often required that the mask be based "upon the 'known' character of the speaker" (288). Mr. Spectator, Donald Bond says, "is consistent with what we know of Addison's tastes and temperament" (Addison 1:1n.2). And Mr. Rambler, according to Richard Schwartz, is "a Johnsonian self-portrait" ("Johnson's 'Mr. Rambler'" 197). As I already noted above, Johnson was often referred to as "the Rambler," "Mr. Rambler," and even "Rambling Sam" (Clifford 73). The Nollekens bust of Johnson in the Victoria and Albert Museum is designated simply *Rambler*.

When the lady in *Rambler* 10 asks about Mr. Rambler's "other name," his "set of friends, his amusements," and "his way of thinking with regard to the living world" (3:52), she is obviously trying to clarify this matter, encouraging Mr. Rambler's creator either to develop Mr. Rambler into a character or to identify himself as Mr. Rambler. Is he a "person now alive, and in town," as she says, or is he a creation? Perhaps he is a creation who pretends to be alive and in town? Johnson's/Mr. Rambler's response to the lady seems not particularly helpful, as he declares she "is never to know my name" (3:52). Of course, if her "other name" is "Hester Mulso" then she does learn his other name eventually—if that name is "Samuel Johnson." Mulso (or her creation) articulates a widespread desire, or she at least voices a desire Johnson represents as widespread. Some three months later Mr. Rambler reports that his readers, having "from the performances of my predecessors, established an idea of unconnected essays," seem to believe that "all future authors" are "under a necessity of conforming" to "their system" (3:128). These readers (real? invented?) are "angry that the Rambler did not, like the Spectator, introduce himself to the acquaintance of the publick" and provide at the beginning of his series "an account of his own birth and studies, and enumeration of his adventures, and a description of his physiognomy" (3:129). These readers fail to consider that Johnson's essays may not be "unconnected," and his aim may not be Addison and Steele's—thus suggesting the difference for Johnson's other readers.

Johnson's creation of such an elusive, on-the-verge-of-disappearing character, eidolon, self-representation—vaguely recalling Mr. Spectator, a re-calling "he" declines—is illuminated by the final essay. In *Rambler* 208 we learn that every "nameless writer" is allowed to assume a "mask" that (Castiglione is called upon to say) "confers a right of acting and speaking with less restraint" (5:317).

Furthermore, "even when the wearer happens to be known," he "cannot be rigorously called to justify those sallies or frolicks which his disguise must prove him desirous to conceal" (5:318).

Such an apology is attributable to an implied author that we now may name "Johnson," who may be distinct from the "historical" Johnson, and who is suggesting that he actually was praising "Mr. Rambler," not himself. The writer in disguise, even when his disguise fails, is not strictly himself and is therefore allowed "less restraint." At the same time, this distance or difference between Johnson and "Johnson" and Mr. Rambler is undone by an unwillingness to erase the writer's identity and responsibility, for Johnson/Mr. Rambler also states that "I have always thought it the duty of an anonymous author to write, as if he expected hereafter to be known" (5:318). Strictly speaking, "Mr. Rambler" must name an "anonymous" author whose mask displays the provisional intention not to be known and not to be unknown.

This sort of strategy—being of the world but not in it—is motivated in part by Johnson's understanding of how rhetorical power is most effectively exercised. In *Rambler* 20 the ideal state of an author is compared to that of "the oriental monarchs," who used "to hide themselves in gardens and palaces" in order to make their edicts more powerful—a practice, we are told, that authors should emulate, "for men would not more patiently submit to be taught, than commanded, by one known to have the same follies and weaknesses with themselves" (3:74–75). *Rambler* 87 similarly concludes that "dead counsellors are . . . most instructive, because they are heard with patience and reverence" (4:96–97), a position supported, ironically, by a quotation from *The Spectator*, whose dead authors are heard so patiently and reverently that Johnson refuses to bring Mr. Rambler to life, or threatens to make him disappear. We cannot say Mr. Rambler is dead, but Mulso's lady, as we have seen, does wonder if he is "a person now alive"—and she receives no direct answer.

Thus, Bloom's notion of the author's inviolate self and Weinbrot's theory of the persona (formulated within the tradition of classical rhetoric) may perhaps be usefully supplemented in the case of Johnson/Mr. Rambler by Michel Foucault's now-familiar description of the poststructural "author-function." As Foucault says, "The writing subject cancels out the signs of his particular individuality," so that "the mark of the writer is reduced to nothing more than the singularity of his absence" (143).[10] The idea that the writer "cancels out" his individuality in order to create a productive space seems particularly suggestive in the case of Johnson, who links and divorces self and persona, and courts and dismisses the audience. Although Johnson fashioned himself into the first great author to acknowledge his dependence upon publishers and the public ("No man but a blockhead ever wrote except for money," we remember), he also resisted direct presentation of himself, blocking and interrupting his own attempts to write an autobiography and to keep a journal, even as the public's fascination with his personal life grew.[11] The "many particulars" of his life that he had been able to commit to paper "at different times, in a desultory manner," were largely "consigned by him to the flames, a few days before his death," according to Boswell (1:25). In this light, one of Johnson's first "appearances" as an author seems richly emblematic. Asked to dine with Edward Cave and Dr. Walter Harte, Johnson was "dressed so shabbily, that he did not choose to appear" (Boswell 1:163n.1). So the absent author ate behind a screen, removed from those with whom he was having dinner.

At the same time, however, Johnson as a human being has seemed far from absent. Many readers would agree with Alvin Kernan that "Johnson seems to us totally real, almost overwhelmingly so" (109). This "totally real" Johnson is the textual product of many people, including of course Boswell, but Johnson's own role in the vividness of his absence is important. "To imagine writing as absence," Foucault says, "keeps alive, in the grey light of neutralization, the interplay of those representations that formed a particular image of the author" (145). Johnson, who has Mr. Rambler call himself "a kind of neutral being" (3:98), seems acutely aware of "writing as absence" and the resulting "interplay" of our imagining.

The specific context of Mr. Rambler's declaration of nonalignment has to do with his gender, as he claims to "place" himself "between the sexes," able to adjudicate objectively in disputes between men and women. Although Mr. Spectator also claims neutrality, he is especially concerned with the "fashionable follies" of women. There are none, he claims early on, "to whom this paper will be more useful than to the female world" (1:46–47). Johnson confirms and no doubt helps to create his readers' disappointed expectations that *The Rambler* will follow *The Spectator*'s sexual orientation. As Mr. Rambler reports in the twenty-third issue, he has been faulted for failing to imitate "the politeness of his predecessors, having hitherto neglected to take the ladies under his protection, and give them rules for the just opposition of colours, and the proper dimensions of ruffles and pinners" (3:129).

One might argue that this depiction significantly revises or misreads Johnson's precursor, which did comment on such concerns as ribbons and ruffles, but only to direct women readers toward more substantive matters. In *Spectator* 265, a typical example, Addison concludes his analysis of the current fashion of colored hoods by exhorting women to "be as industrious to cultivate their minds, as they are to adorn their bodies" (2:533). Johnson's version of *The Spectator* overlooks such endings, focusing instead on such passages as Mr. Spectator's comparison of women to caterpillars who have been "in a kind of moulting season" (2:531). Having cast away "great quantities of ribbon, lace, and cambric," reducing "in some measure" "that part of the human figure to the beautiful globular form which is natural to it," the women now have turned their thoughts "upon the other extremity," remembering (in a phrase brimming with innuendo) "if you light your fire at both ends the middle will shift for itself." Even by eighteenth-century standards, this portrait—woman as insect, firewood, "globular form," fashion slave—is unflattering. Throughout the essay Addison applauds the superior beauty of English women, and he advises them to be *equally* industrious in improving mind and body, not to prefer intellectual cultivation. Thus one could easily argue that Addison does much to perpetuate the emphasis upon appearance that he purports to discourage—and that Johnson's "misreading" is usefully revealing.

What is perhaps most conventional and yet disturbing about the vision of women generally promulgated by Addison and Steele and their contributors is the assignment of certain demeaning frailties to feminine nature rather than to societal influence. A rather mild instance related to the foregoing example occurs in *Spectator* 15, when Mr. Spectator remarks, "I have often reflected with myself on this unaccountable humour in womankind, of being smitten with everything that is showy and superficial, and on the numberless evils that befall the sex from this light, fantastical disposition" (1:66–67). He even knows of a suitor able to win his beloved by adding "a supernumerary lace," and he further reminds us that even Virgil's fierce Amazonian warrior, Camilla, was susceptible to a Trojan soldier's fancy clothes.

For Johnson, such a "humour" is not "unaccountable" at all. *Rambler* 66 asks, for instance, how "can we endeavour to persuade the ladies, that the time spent at the toilet is lost in vanity, when they have every moment some new conviction, that their interest is more effectually promoted by a ribband well disposed, than by the brightest act of virtue?" (3:353). The idea that cultural directives largely create the peculiar frailties of women occurs repeatedly in *The Rambler*. Poor Bellaria finds, in *Rambler* 191, that she has almost frightened Mr. Trip away by quoting Dryden (5:238). In *Rambler* 85, Myrtylla's aunt "snatches" away her book when she tries to read, and tears her paper when she tries to write (4:80). Lady Bustle sees no need to educate her daughters, having contracted her own cares into "a narrow space." Household chores are the sole meaning of life for her. Ironically, Cornelia finds she cannot help in the kitchen because of Lady Bustle's eccentric spelling. Are such ladies, Cornelia asks, "the great patterns of our sex" (3:279)? Generosa, who is Johnson's creation and cannot, from her fictional vantage point, attribute these and other such efforts in favor of women's education to Mr. Rambler, directs his attention in number 126 to "your great predecessor, the Spectator," who "endeavoured to diffuse among his female readers a desire of knowledge." Mr. Rambler, she charges, has not been "equally attentive to the ladies." Yet, although Generosa has been impressed with the *Spectator*'s encouragement of knowledge, she has apparently learned little from it. She tells of asking an astronomer a civil question and being rebuffed by his condescending answer, but it is obvious that she asked the question not to gain any insight but rather, condescendingly, to allow the scholar to discourse "of the only subject on which I believed him able to speak with propriety" (4:311)—practising some stereotyping of her own.

It is obviously difficult and dangerous to generalize about a work as varied and enormous as *The Spectator* (or *The Rambler* for that matter), but I would agree with Pat Rogers' assertion that "Addison wanted to educate women so that they should not corrupt or weaken the male strain. They are to be made sensible enough not to irritate men of feeling" (96). Johnson, or Mr. Rambler, is not "equally attentive to the ladies," we may posit, because he generally has a more equal conception of women. This hypothesis is in fact in accord with other recent assessments of Johnson's attitude toward women, looking beyond his reported conversational grenades. Isobel Grundy for instance has shown how Johnson practiced a generous patronage of women writers and intellectuals ("Patron"). According to Katherine Rogers, Johnson's attitude toward women was "in general benign and rather enlightened" (9). Other students of Johnson have been even more positive, seeing him as "an outspoken defender of women's rights" and even an outright feminist.[12] We know that Johnson's sensitivity toward prostitutes was extraordinary, both in life and in fiction, even by Johnsonian standards of sympathy. The histories of Misella in *Ramblers* 170 and 171 and of Zosima in *Rambler* 12 are especially affecting. Other eighteenth-century moralists, as Terry Castle has observed, seem to have ignored the want and hunger that motivated prostitution, blaming instead uncontrolled passion and moral weakness. Further, we know that *Rambler* 107, by Joseph Simpson, was probably responsible for the creation of Magdelen Hospital for unwed mothers. Introducing the letters in that issue, Mr. Rambler tells us that the combination of comic and serious letters being presented is a response to the "unavoidable comparison of my performances with those of my predecessors" (4:204) and the resulting charge of excessive uniformity. Although the somber Mr. Rambler cannot bring himself to unite "gay and solemn themes" (4:205), he does offer contrasting letters from correspondents, thus again rejecting and following his predecessor.

This gesture describes Johnson's relationship to Addison and Steele in this arena as well as others: he both extends and denies his precursor's "feminism." Johnson's attitude is exemplified by *Rambler* 39, a moving analysis of the way women's peculiar physical discomforts have been exacerbated by social conventions that "seem to have almost excluded them [women] from content," as "the custom of the world seems to have been formed in a kind of conspiracy against them" (3:211).

What does the status of "Mr. Rambler" contribute to Johnson's stance in this regard? In *Rambler* 109 a correspondent informs Mr. Rambler that "you have not yet exhausted the whole stock of human infelicity," and he imagines "the Rambler snuffing his candle, rubbing his spectacles, stirring his fire, locking out interruption, and settling himself in his easy chair that he may enjoy a new calamity without disturbance" (4:215). The correspondent is uncertain whether Mr. Rambler intends his writings "as antidotal to the levity and merriment" of his "rivals," or whether he imagines he can "warble out" his "groan" with "uncommon elegance or energy" (4:215, 216). Johnson places Mr. Rambler in a comical light here, and it is difficult not to see Mr. Rambler's claim of neutrality in a similarly absurd way, as his evidence subverts his assertion. He is able, he says, to "hear the vociferations of either sex without catching any of the fire from those that utter them" because he has "found, by long experience, that a man will sometimes rage at his wife, when in reality his mistress has offended him; and a lady complain of the cruelty of her husband, when she has no other enemy than bad cards" (3:99). Despite the structural balance here, "a man" and then "a lady," the blame is placed on the feminine in both cases (the offending mistress, the irrational cardplayer). Ironically, Mr. Rambler's "neutrality" was presented as the effect of his recognition that "as the faculty of writing has been chiefly a masculine endowment, the reproach of making the world miserable has been always thrown upon the women" (3:98)—a reproach, it appears, he now unintentionally has nurtured.

Mr. Rambler appears particularly ludicrous and distanced from Johnson in *Rambler* 20, where he castigates those who in

who painted the lion

their writing "affect the style and the name of ladies" (3:111). Mr. Rambler's reaction—that "I cannot always withhold some expression of anger . . . when I happen to find . . . a woman has a beard"—seems quite odd, given his claim two essays earlier to be an aged philosopher in total control of his passions (3:99), not to mention the letter from Zosima in *Rambler* 12 or the one from Cleora in *Rambler* 15. Both these ladies would have had Johnson's beard, had he worn one. In fact, *Rambler* 20, based on the universal "aversion from all kinds of disguise," occurs in an essay series full of impersonations and is of course itself attributed to "Mr. Rambler." How should we explain such "hostile passions" against sexual deception by one who puts on so many print dresses, unless we imagine Johnson laughing at Mr. Rambler?

Johnson's illustration in *Rambler* 14 of the "manifest and striking contrariety between the life of an author and his writings" also deserves to be viewed in terms of the following comment in the same essay:

> A sudden intruder into the closet of an author would perhaps feel equal indignation with the officer, who having long solicited admission to the presence of Sardanapulus, saw him not consulting upon laws, enquiring into grievances, or modelling armies, but employed in feminine amusements, and directing the ladies in their work. (3:75)

The bearded women, the objects of Mr. Rambler's attack in *Rambler* 20, are like Sardanapalus. In taking up their feminine pens, those unsuccessful authors in *Rambler* 20 seem to lose their penises. It is, Mr. Rambler chides them, "much easier not to write like a man, than to write like a woman" (3:112). Becoming "not . . . like a man," they become aberrations, neutral beings between the sexes, in equipoise—in the condition Mr. Rambler assumes and castigates. Sardanapalus and the bearded women may expose the disabling effect of the feminine upon the masculine but, just as importantly, these instances also point toward the necessity of disguise and self-suppression, which we have traced through the opening essays. Johnson apparently begins with the assumption that an intrusion "into the closet of an author" will as a matter of course produce some damaging evidence, and he casts this evidence in terms of sexual negation. Even though aversion to disguise is "universally diffused, and incessantly in action" (3:110), secrecy seems to be a necessity: disguise must itself be disguised. Thus the epistolary transvestites, failing to keep their sexual and textual identities in the closet, deserve Mr. Rambler's scorn both for appearing as women (descending to the feminine) and for not appearing as women (retaining signs of the masculine).

A similar stance governs Johnson's most extensive consideration in *The Rambler* of courtship and marriage, the correspondence of Hymenaeus and Tranquilla, which dramatically illustrates the difference between *The Spectator's* essentially optimistic presentation of patriarchal marriage and *The Rambler's* troubled view of marital equality. Steele in *Spectator* 490 considers marriage "an Institution calculated for a constant scene of as much Delight as our Being is capable of." When people keep their marital commitments, "the most indifferent Circumstances administer Delight," and their condition is "an endless Source of new Gratifications" (4:237).

From Johnson's perspective such idealism is especially dangerous, creating expectations that can only be disappointed. For Hymenaeus and Tranquilla even the most fundamental considerations of marrying are problematic, as they both encounter potential mates whose sexual polarity seems questionable. In *Rambler* 119 Tranquilla divulges her unhappy experiences with, among other suitors, Flosculus, whose name appropriately means "little flower," and Venustulus, whose name, also apt, points to the goddess of feminine charm. Hymenaeus had revealed in *Rambler* 113 his initial attraction to Ferocula, a woman marvelously "free from the weakness and timidity of female minds" (4:238). But this lack of feminine frailty, he soon discovers, has been offset by some disturbingly aggressive, masculine behaviors. When Hymenaeus finally discovers Ferocula disputing ferociously with a chairman over six pence, he leaves her in disgust, observing that she needs no assistance from a man. In case we have missed Johnson's point, Hymenaeus also meets Camilla, who despises her own sex and thereby repulsively "advances to the borders of virility" (4:250), as well as Misothea, who "scarcely condescended to make tea, but for the linguist, the geometrician, the astronomer, or the poet" (4:239). Like the "Queen of the Amazons," Misothea will adopt a submissively feminine posture only toward "the hero who could conquer her in single combat"—that is, by disputation. Sexual ambiguity is more than an object of ridicule here: one of the most horrifying sentences in Johnson's canon is Hymenaeus's conclusion that Camilla's posture is "soliciting assault," inviting and perhaps even authorizing the violent impress of her biological sex upon her.

If we burst in upon a general, an author, or anyone else, Johnson implies we may well find their identities, including their sexual statuses, in question. Johnson, like those feminists who have embraced deconstruction, reconsiders the essential polarity of sexuality as well as of author and persona, precursor and follower. The implications of this version of sexual equality, or equivalence, are sobering, especially in light of Johnson's definition of marriage in *Rambler* 18 as "the strictest type of perpetual friendship" (3:103). In *Spectator* 15 Addison presents a similar depiction of the ideal marriage with his portrait of Aurelia, whose husband is "her bosom friend and companion in her solitudes" (1:68). But Addison's opposing image, of the miserable marriage of Fulvia, tends to contradict this idea of marriage as friendship. Fulvia "considers her husband as her steward, and looks upon discretion and good housewifery as little domestic virtues unbecoming a woman of quality." Aurelia's husband may have extended friendship to her, but there is no question who should be handling the "little domestic virtues," who should be occupying the role of steward.

Johnson perceives more clearly the radical implications of defining marriage as friendship. This equation, despite its familiarity, undoes conventional oppositions. Marriage, involving sexuality, hierarchy, alterity, conquest, and sacrament, is identified with friendship, which is platonic, equal, isomorphic, unifying, and secular. There is of course a profound truth in the dismantling of these two categories, but if marriage encompasses the same ground as friendship, then what is the difference?

Such a lack of difference plays a crucial role in the resolution of Hymenaeus and Tranquilla's marriage sequence in *The Rambler*, which is in effect a revision of Addison's depiction of the blissful marriage. Their assessment of the marital happiness to come, completing the series of letters on their courtship experiences, is that their marriage may "probably be less tasteless" than most (5:123). This less-than-enthusiastic outlook stems from their belief that they are "less deceived" in connubial hopes. Expecting to be less unhappy because one expects not to be so happy is obviously more of a cancelling out than a positive emotion. Given their piety and the struggles they have endured in courtship, their conclusion is especially striking. Indeed, Tranquilla's name may be seen as more of a negation or stasis than a pleasing alterity; and Hymenaeus's name, suggesting not only marriage but also the mark of female virginity, points to what he lacks. He exists, he says, in a state of "frozen celibacy," a neutral being like Mr. Rambler, without an anatomical or a metaphorical hymen to designate his sexual status, mocked by his name. Together their names make a "tranquil marriage," and it is difficult to imagine in this "less tasteless" match, with such a lack of difference, much more than the erasure of celibacy.

Addison anticipates to some extent Johnson's perception of the restlessness such harmony effects. Aurelia and her husband "often go into company that they may return with the greater delight to one another; and sometimes live in town, not to enjoy it so properly as to grow weary of it," thereby enhancing the pleasures of their retirement (1:82). Johnson echoes and goes beyond this recognition, as Hymenaeus and Tranquilla acknowledge "that however our eyes may yet sparkle, and our hearts bound at the presence of each other, the time of listlessness and satiety, or peevishness and discontent must come at last, in which we shall be driven for relief to shews and recreations" (5:123). For Johnson the decision to marry approaches another situation of equipoise. As Hymenaeus and Tranquilla say, "There are advantages to be enjoyed in marriage," and "there are inconveniencies likewise to be endured" (5:121). Hymenaeus and Tranquilla thus "rejoice" in "stores of novelty yet unexhausted" and "gratifications yet untasted," even though these are clearly temporary and uncertain reprieves. Further, their vow that "artifice and concealment are to be banished for ever" from their relationship will certainly be difficult to keep, given the pervasiveness and even necessity of disguise (5:124). Their openness may in fact be said to stem from a kind of poverty, as they have "nothing to conceal." Their letter concludes with a final equipoise, in which they imagine a future of "extensive happiness" that "spreads by degrees into the boundless regions of eternity" (5:124–25). Yet they also affirm that if "we are doomed to give one instance more of the uncertainty of human discernment" (which of course eventually they must to some degree), then they are comforted to have "sought happiness" not in each other's arms precisely but "only in the arms of virtue" (5:125).

Hymenaeus and Tranquilla thus adopt a kind of defensive posture not unlike Mr. Rambler's, in which security is sought through the contraction and discipline of desire, turning it toward an object that is not present (eternity, virtue). Hymenaeus and Tranquilla's marriage is based on a kind of conflict partially suppressed, as they count on "the gentle effervescence of contrary qualities" to fuel their relationship, arising from both a "general resemblance" and a stimulating diversity (5:124, 123). Johnson's term for a such a relationship is of course *"concordia discors,"* an impossible unity of difference.

If Bloom's vision of the Oedipal conflict that strong writers face helps us see Johnson's sensitivity to the "hazardous state" of an author, we must also acknowledge now that following after a famous predecessor is not the only or even the most important problem that Johnson perceives. I think it is clear that Bloom's special insight, his profound commitment to the authorial self, seeking out those authors who speak "most grandly, for the isolate selfhood" (*Map* 63), necessarily tends to obscure other conceptions of the self and other motivations. Johnson discloses an acute awareness of the permeability and hiddenness of authorial and sexual boundaries—an awareness that is both disturbing and encouraging in its implications regarding self-fashioning. The limits of Bloom's vision can be further clarified by looking at his own response to Johnson. In other words, if Bloom supplies a way to read Johnson, does Johnson provide a way to read (beyond) Bloom?

In *Dr. Samuel Johnson and James Boswell,* one of the over two hundred volumes in the Modern Critical Views series he is editing, Bloom observes in his introduction that "we all of us have a favorite writer; as I grow older, Johnson is mine, as Pope was Johnson's" (6). Bloom's affection for Johnson is interesting in itself (what would Johnson think?), but why does he add the comparison, "as Pope was Johnson's"? The implied genealogy is clear: Pope → Johnson → Bloom. Bloom, who is certainly one of the greatest critics of our century, identifies Johnson as "the central Western literary critic," "the strongest critic in the varied history of Western literary culture," the "greatest of critics" (viii, 1, 3). Johnson is, in other words, the critic's most formidable precursor today. Does this alignment mean that Bloom, if he is himself a "strong" critic, is obliged to struggle against his "favorite," strategically misreading him? Is there any evidence of such an effort?

Perhaps Bloom's most obvious defense against Johnson's overwhelming influence can be witnessed in his volume's title, *Dr. Samuel Johnson and James Boswell.* Johnson did not use his honorary doctorate, and for many years now virtually all Johnsonians have regarded "Dr. Johnson" as the mark of a regrettable stereotype—Johnson as the eccentric, comical "Dr. Johnson" of Boswell's *Life*: a character, a caricature, but not the author of works deserving their own careful reading. One established scholar has even compared the way Johnsonians feel about "Dr. Johnson" to the way blacks felt about "Negro" in the 1960s and 1970s (Vance 9). Thus, although Bloom calls the *Lives of the Poets* Johnson's "greatest" accomplishment, he quickly asserts that "everything about this work is peculiar"; it is "a very odd collection of the British poets"; and Johnson "mostly shrugs them off, even when he had suggested them" (4). Bloom focuses on one of the most marginal lives as if it were typical, and even manages to cast a Shandean air over Johnson's endeavor by drawing our attention to the oddities of Yalden's verse ("Alas, poor Yalden!" Bloom says). Further, Bloom passes over Pope, Johnson's "masterpiece," to deal with the more colorful Swift, whose "extraordinary nightmare" "unnerved" Johnson (6, 5). Although Bloom does applaud Johnson's criticism of Gray, the only example offered is the judgment that Gray's odes "are but cucumbers after all"—a comment that in fact appears in Boswell (4:13). Bloom underscores the comedy of this "criticism" by pointing out that Johnson means the "ungainly and rough" British cucumber, which does have the shape, perhaps, of a Gray pindaric. The clearest deflection of Johnson's force, swerving from his own writing, is the very act of pairing him with Boswell here. Even though A. R. Ammons, John Le Carrè, Gershom Scholem, and Gore Vidal are assigned separate volumes in the series, Boswell (author of "the finest literary biography") and "Dr. Johnson" (the West's greatest critic) are inextricably bound together, linked arm-in-arm forever on the volume's cover, as each remains a reflection of the other. Bloom, who is himself engaged in writing prefaces on a Johnsonian scale, who in fact often appears to quote from memory (in Johnsonian fashion), would appear to be uniquely positioned to appreciate Johnson's *Lives*. But the effect of his discussion is a synecdochic substitution of "Dr. Johnson" for Johnson, repressing Johnson's achievement.

A more subtle aspect of Bloom's defense against Johnson's continuing dominance is to limit the range of his writing. "Johnson's great achievement," Bloom asserts, "was his criticism" (7)—which is suffused, so we supposedly see, by oddity and peculiarity. Although he does not mention it, Bloom is of course unable to deny that Johnson worked in virtually every genre available to him, but Bloom can say "it is accurate to remark that *The Vanity of Human Wishes, Rasselas,* and the more general essays are memorable as extensions of Johnsonian literary criticism or wisdom literature" (7–8). Thus Johnson's other writings are valuable as literary criticism or as "wisdom literature," but in his opening paragraph Bloom has already shown us, or said "Johnson shows us," that "criticism, as a literary art, joins itself to the ancient genre of wisdom writing" (1). By collapsing Johnson's work into the single category of criticism-and-wisdom-literature, Bloom is able to assert that Johnson's thought "is descended from Koheleth (Ecclesiastes) and Jesus Ben Sirach (Ecclesiasticus)" (1). Given the importance of Jewish theology in his own criticism, Bloom would appear to be reading Johnson, the whimsically encyclopedic critic, into the position of Bloom's (undeclared) precursor in another way.

Having circumscribed Johnson within Koheleth, Bloom distances and weakens his favorite writer further by claiming "Johnson is so strong a writer, that he nearly achieves the metaleptic reversal of making us believe that the author of Ecclesiastes has read deeply in Samuel Johnson" (1). While Johnson might well be flattered (and astonished) by this statement, Bloom's reversal ends up qualifying Johnson's achievement: in a critical system that values originality and selfhood, Johnson ultimately fails to distinguish himself from his influence. "Sometimes I find myself," Bloom somewhat implausibly says, "reading Ecclesiastes aloud, and become confused, believing that I am reading *Rasselas*" (1–2). In identifying Johnson with his influence, by which he says Johnson's mind was "altered permanently," Bloom substitutes an Old Testament precursor for the eighteenth-century Christian work that Johnson said did transform his thought, Law's *Serious Call*. His misreading, shaping Johnson into Bloom's subdued forerunner, glides over Johnson's Christianity and his moral rhetoric, the serious purpose of his writing.

If Bloom draws our attention to rhetoric as the art of psychic defense, he may also distract us from the persuasive intent of Johnson's work. Dividing *The Rambler* within itself, distancing Mr. Rambler from his correspondents, obscuring "Mr. Rambler" and "Johnson," playing pardon against praise, entertainment against instruction, Time against the audience, male against female—these are strategies designed not only to usurp the patriarchs of the essay series, but more importantly to shape resistent readers' views of another Patriarch that Johnson aims to follow. To understand better how Johnson uses the room created by his engagement with *The Spectator*, I turn in the next part to a more direct consideration of the working out of Johnson's rhetoric (as the art of persuasion) within another sort of deconstructive vision.

3

A Difference in Nothing:
Johnson and Derrida

To proceed from one truth to another, and connect
distant propositions by regular consequences, is the
great prerogative of man. Independent and unconnected
sentiments flashing upon the mind in quick succession,
may, for a time, delight by their novelty, but they differ
from systematical reasoning as single notes from
harmony, as glances of lightening from the radiance of
the sun.

—*Rambler* 158

"Wander in the Wrong Way"

Despite the celebration in *Rambler* 158 of "the great prerogative
of man," it has become a critical commonplace that Johnson, the
demolisher of so many complacent profundities, was inveterately
skeptical of systematic thought. William Edinger says for instance,
"We must remind ourselves of the inclusive nature of Johnson's
eclecticism and of the unsystematic nature of his thought," which
together "define his limitations as a theorist" and sometimes lead
him into "logical inconsistencies" (171). Robert DeMaria similarly
sees Johnson as "a thinker who was not systematic by any account"
and whose *Dictionary* "with all its inconsistencies and counter-
points" stands as "a record" of his mind (*Learning* 90–91). In fact,

*his thought is not
unsystematic.*

all "codified philosophies," DeMaria says, including even skepticism, are "an object of scorn in the *Dictionary*" (83). Leopold Damrosch likewise points to Johnson's "profound skepticism about theoretical systems" (*Uses* 33), and James Boyd White confidently asserts that the *Ramblers* are "not offered as building blocks of a theoretical system" (152–53). Robert Voitle goes so far as to say "only a fool would expect to find an elaborate, regular theory" underlying Johnson's ethical assertions (125).

Of course, we should note that many of Johnson's inconsistencies are exposed by using as evidence various reports of his conversational remarks—which may be misremembered, or perhaps even fabricated, or may capture Johnson playing a role to stimulate or even aggravate his audience.[1] We should also acknowledge that some outstanding work has been based on the idea of a fundamental coherence in Johnson's thought. I think immediately of William R. Keast's "Theoretical Foundations of Johnson's Criticism," or Isobel Grundy's study of the idea of "greatness," to pick only two examples separated by decades and diverse interests. Yet even when Johnson's critics are providing exceedingly useful organizations of his thought, they often tend to deny the coherence their analysis reveals. Nicholas Hudson asserts for instance that he is "disclosing no single truth about Johnson," that he has "no overriding theory"; and yet his work impressively demonstrates how Johnson embraced the doctrines of "Christian epicureanism" (3, 66–85). Although obviously this is not the place for an exhaustive review of the contradictions Johnsonians may have exhibited in revealing Johnson's contradictions, I would like to look closely at one characteristic example from Hudson because it illustrates how even Johnson's best readers have been too willing to perceive his inconsistencies. Before I argue for the value of looking for a "regular theory" underlying Johnson's assertions, it may be prudent to explain how so large a consensus might have formed at odds with that thesis. Moreover, I want to examine this particular instance because if Hudson is correct about it, then the whole project of *The Rambler*, as Johnson articulates it, is based on an assumption denied by Johnson himself.

Discussing Johnson's views on moral judgment, Hudson asks, "How could Johnson give this praise [in *Rambler* 68] to the moral judgment of servants, yet argue elsewhere [in the Vinerian lectures and *Sermons* 4 and 25] that moral truths were far above the comprehension of all but the most enlightened reasoners?" (45). Even if we accept the premise that Johnson necessarily considered servants among the least educated and intelligent, *Rambler* 68 does not in fact claim that servants have a particular acuity in moral judgments. Rather, if we look at the paragraph preceding the one Hudson quotes, we find Johnson observing that "the most authentick witnesses of any man's character are those who know him in his own family, and see him without any restraint, or rule of conduct" in "his private apartments" (3:361). The moral judgments of servants clearly are superior not because their moral judgment as an instrument is superior, as Hudson seems to suggest, but simply because they have a special opportunity to gather evidence.

By the same token, the idea that Johnson questions the ability of "all but the most enlightened reasoners" to perceive moral truths deserves scrutiny. In *Sermon* 4 Johnson does say that the most brilliant reasoners of "the heathen world," despite all their "wild opinions" and "chimerical systems," agreed that charity should rank as the most excellent virtue (14:40); but we do not need "tedious enquiries" to determine "the extent and importance of this great duty," having the "holy Scriptures . . . in our hands." These remarks in isolation may indeed imply that only the most enlightened minds can properly rank charity, but they do not say that only the most enlightened reasoners see the virtue of charity. Johnson seems to me careful to clarify this very point. "Scarcely can any man turn his eyes upon the world, without observing the sudden rotations of affairs, the ruin of the affluent, and the downfall of the high"; and "no man, to whom opportunities of such observations occur, can forbear applying them to his own condition"; therefore, virtually no man can fail to perceive the need for kindness and charity (14:43). Every man should further remember, Johnson says, that those who have forgotten charity, who have sunk into a state of "obdurate wickedness" and may now "scarcely" be considered "any longer human," were "originally formed with passions, and instincts, and reason, like his own"—were formed originally with a comprehension of the virtue of charity.

Johnson's views in these passages thus seem far from contradictory and instead quite consistent with his assertion in *Rambler* 31 that good and evil, in general, are "easily distinguished" (3:172). *The Rambler*, I argue, proceeds from just this assumption—that we know right from wrong, but we still have trouble generating the thoughts and actions we know to be proper, thereby imperiling our souls. While isolated statements may imply some divergence on this issue, Johnson's assertions, read carefully and in context, consistently support the accessibility of valid moral perception. As Johnson says in *Rambler* 155, "Few that wander in the wrong way mistake it for the right" (5:62).

Of course, one consideration only begins to raise the possibility that coherent moral reasoning, in Johnson's estimation, is accessible to almost everyone, and that Johnson's inconsistencies have been too quickly perceived. We should certainly wonder why there has not been more resistance to the idea of a self-contradictory, antisystematic Johnson. Such a Johnson is certainly colorful and interesting, exhibiting an endearing fallibility. Alternately he may be seen as a man of integrity, refusing to compromise his insights in particular situations for the mere sake of consistency, as Patrick O'Flaherty has argued. But, after deconstruction, we have the opportunity to think differently about Johnson's inconsistencies. Perhaps Johnson, who as Bate has shown anticipated Freudian psychology so profoundly (*Samuel Johnson* [1975] 300, 306, 316), is our intellectual contemporary in other ways. Specifically, is it possible that the apparent confusion of Johnson's thought might somehow be the result of some proleptically poststructural insight? Perhaps Johnson contradicts himself because he is deconstructing himself? Such a suggestion is silly if we think of deconstruction strictly as a recent invention, impossible before Derrida. But what if we assume instead that deconstruction names a way of looking at language and the world long available, at least in its fundamental principles? Frederick Bogel is surely correct when he observes that "criticism of eighteenth-century English literature has proven more resis-

tant than criticism of other periods to the incursions of recent theory" (79).[2] In the case of Johnsonians, this relative lack of interest
in deconstruction in particular might in part be explained by the
longstanding focus on Johnson's tendency to dismantle systems
and to speak in contradictions. Why should students of Johnson be
excited by an approach that reveals incoherences, reverses polari-
ties, and dismantles systems? Such a view of their author has long
been familiar, at least since Bertrand Bronson's "Johnson Agonistes" in 1944. Earl Wasserman has said that in *Rasselas* "everything
is bipolar, not multiple," and there is "no clear choice . . . but only
an endless, directionless oscillation between opposites, neither of
which is sufficient or stable" (9, 11); Irvin Ehrenpreis has found
that Johnson's method in *Rasselas* involves "offering a choice of
alternatives and undercutting both" (113); Charles Hinnant has
been repeatedly concerned with Johnson's ambivalences, oppositions, reversals of value, supplements, and deferrals; and James
Boyd White has focused on "Johnson's tendency to think by recognizing and including contraries" (152). These critics might well
appear to be tacitly employing deconstructive themes, or they appear to be perceiving in Johnson something like deconstruction. In
fact, as far back as 1783, a writer for *Parker's General Advertiser*
satirically noted that an "ingenious Lexiphanes," who is Johnson
of course, has undertaken to prove "that several words mean their
opposites" (qtd. in McGuffie 300)—which many today would probably accept as a fair description of deconstruction.

There are of course exceptions to this explicit neglect. Raman
Selden's "Deconstructing the *Ramblers*" openly applies deconstruction to Johnson, confirming the consensus view of Johnson's troubled and chaotic thinking, seeing everywhere "digression, disconti-
nuity, and unresolved contradiction" (271). Although Selden
asserts that Johnson is sometimes "undoing the rigid conceptual
hierarchies his arguments set up" (in other words, that Johnson is
a deconstructive agent), generally Selden argues that Johnson's
discourse exhibits "failures of artistic control" or, more significantly,
"lapses of logocentric will," "the necessary traces of the Other." In
other words Johnson is the victim, as we all must be, of the gaps
and slippages inherent within language (270).

69

Another exception is Jean Hagstrum's "Samuel Johnson Among the Deconstructionists," which identifies (much to our surprise, Hagstrum expects) two points of agreement between Johnson and "the deconstructionists." Johnson, Hagstrum entertainingly argues, would have generally been in sympathy with the idea of criticism "as within literature, not outside of it looking in" (147), and Johnson also would have appreciated the use of a new and ambitious critical terminology. Hagstrum considers it "a pity that so few contemporary critics have seen fit to wrestle with Johnson," for he "may be regarded as one of the most original and persistent deconstructionists in our language" (144). Hagstrum does not pursue this tantalizing observation, opening, he acknowledges, "only very small doors" (150) between Johnson and deconstruction. "I simply do not dare," he says, to "juxtapose Johnson and Derrida" (139).

Playing Voitle's fool, going where no Hagstrum has dared to juxtapose, in this chapter I propose to consider the possibility that some "elaborate, regular theory" does underlie Johnson's assertions and that *The Rambler* shows us Johnson exercising "the great prerogative of man," systematical reasoning. I am going to get to that point by provisionally postulating that we might call this theory "deconstruction"—or, rather, that after deconstruction we might now be in a position to see the antifoundational foundation of Johnson's thinking, as if we have now discovered the 3-D glasses allowing us to view properly a movie made long ago.

This hypothesis (not to ruin the suspense) does not hold up entirely, although it goes farther that we might have imagined and ultimately illuminates both Johnson and Derrida. More specifically, having examined Johnson's philosophy of language and his ideas of freedom and meaning in the light (or darkness visible) of deconstruction, we will have a better idea what Johnson's underlying theory might be based on, if it exists, and how it might be presented. I will argue that this theory is based on or derived from our perception of life's vacuity, and that we get to it by thinking through, in several senses, something very much like deconstruction. Further, I try to explain why Johnson's theory of everything must be presented in such a way that we miss it, at least at first, at least long enough to forget we already know it. To see this theory in operation, I will then return to where the previous chapter's sequential analysis became stratified, with *Rambler* 5, and will consider closely how Johnson's underlying theory, which we are missing, is at work in that essay and the three following. Finally, as in the previous chapter, I suggest how the series as a whole supports my findings by referring to a distributed sampling of essays. In sum, I argue here that Johnson's systematic philosophy of language, of time and space, of consciousness, and of moral discipline—which exhibits some interesting convergences and illuminating contrasts with deconstruction—shapes everything in *The Rambler*, from the title to the final word.

"The Daughters of the Earth"

Although Derrida and company have been with us for decades now, and we are thus in some sense situated "after deconstruction," it nonetheless seems reasonable, if we are going to trace Johnson's reflection in it, to say what is meant here by that term—recognizing of course that a diversity of acts have been committed in its name, and further that deconstruction by definition stipulates the necessary inaccuracy and incompleteness of any act of defining. As Gregory Jay says, "deconstruction" is "now an admittedly indeterminate nominative" (*America* xi). (If deconstruction is correct, it always was.) Given the sometimes baffling gymnastics we have seen involved in such efforts to define the undefinable, to write the unwritable, J. Hillis Miller's recent definition at the outset of *The Ethics of Reading* seems an especially attractive starting point for this doomed but necessary move. "Deconstruction is nothing," Miller says, "more or less than good reading as such" (10). This reassuring description, part of Miller's attack on those who have charged deconstruction with negativity or nihilism, seems more and more outrageously comic, even cynical, as we proceed through Miller's book and repeated encounters with what emerges as "the law of unreadability." As Miller puts it, summarizing (almost chanting it seems) the insights of Paul de Man:

> The failure to read takes place inexorably within the text
> itself. The reader must enact this failure in his or her
> own reading. Getting it right always means being forced
> to reenact once more the necessity of getting it wrong.
> Each reader must repeat the error the text denounces
> and then commits again. (53)

In these terms we have achieved "nothing more or less than good reading" precisely when we realize we have failed to read. Perhaps this is not nihilism, as Miller vigorously insists, but it does tend to be depressing to those who like to think of accomplishments in positive terms.[3]

Similarly, Miller joins those who forcefully deny that Derrida or de Man "has ever asserted the freedom of the reader to make the text mean anything he or she wants it to mean" (10). But Miller fails to explain immediately or clearly that the inaccuracy of this charge has to do with mistaken notions of the freedom of the reader and the making of meaning. The reader, from the point of view of Derridean deconstruction, isn't free, and the meaning is never really made. There is only, Derrida says, "the illusory autonomy of a discourse or a consciousness whose hypostasis is to be deconstructed" (*Positions* 28) as we "pass beyond man and humanism" ("Structure" 265)—into what, if not determinism? If the reader cannot make the text mean anything he or she wants, is that because the reader is not an autonomous subject? Consciousness, according to Derrida, is nothing more or less than "a determination of an effect within a system which is no longer that of presence but of differance" (*Margins* 16). And "differance," which is that "trace," that "no-thing," that "gap" between signified and signifier, is "related no less to what is called future than to what is called the past" (*Margins* 18). Both past and future are as much functions of absence, of difference and deferral, as the present. Not only consciousness and time but also space is constituted by "the simulacrum of a presence that dislocates itself, displaces itself," and "properly has no site" (*Margins* 24). Deconstruction, positing a space and time and individuality of "the mirage" (*Grammatology* 62), might therefore be viewed provisionally as an especially potent and thorough skepticism (not nihilism), concerned with the reader's lack of unmediated autonomy, with the subject under erasure, different from itself—and not with his or her rampant freedom.

As Art Berman puts it, "The space that Foucault, Lacan, and Derrida open up between the Saussurian signified and signifier . . . becomes the space between language and reality as well as between desire and its object" (225). This productive "space" or "gap" or "differance" between binary oppositions (like speech/writing, man/woman, inside/outside) allows meaning to be put into play, into motion. Such oppositions are, as John Sheriff says, "irreducible," making "everything in opposition mutually dependent on each other for meaning" (46). Or according to Christopher Norris, "The Saussurian 'bar' between signifier and signified—that which creates the arbitrary nature of the sign—is also the law which immutably decrees the unfulfilment of desire in pursuit of its ever-changing object" (114). Within this "play of differences" as Derrida calls it (*Margins* 11), we are always forced to make choices that can be revealed to be arbitrary. Because we are unable to unite unavoidable oppositions, we must expect that something is always left out, or in, or over.

It perhaps may seem that more than warp drive and time travel would be required to get from this point (or mirage of a point) to Johnson, but the general critical agreement regarding the profundity of Johnson's skepticism alone would seem to encourage at least some further consideration. So let us turn to a particularly telling and characteristic passage in which Johnson is talking about consciousness, time, and space, the opening of *Rambler* 41:

> So few of the hours of life are filled up with objects adequate to the mind of man, and so frequently are we in want of present pleasure or employment, that we are forced to have recourse every moment to the past and future for supplemental satisfactions, and relieve the vacuities of our being, by recollection of former passages, or anticipation of events to come. (3:221)

Samuel Johnson after Deconstruction

This sweeping first sentence is sobering, disturbing, and even depressing, but is it in any sense deconstructive? It does involve Johnson in a kind of double writing, undermining while seeming to repeat the sentiment of the essay's motto, from Martial:

> Nulla recordanti lux est ingrata gravisque,
> Nulla fuit cujus non meminisse velit.
> Ampliat aetatis spatium sibi vir bonus, hoc est
> Vivere bis, vitâ posse priore frui.

F. Lewis's translation, added to the 1752 edition, stands between (literally and semantically) Johnson's and Martial's opening sentences:

> No day's remembrance shall the good regret,
> Nor wish one bitter moment to forget;
> They stretch the limits of this narrow span,
> And, by enjoying, live past life again.

For Lewis, the stretching of life by memory is "living past life again," a repetition, but Martial refers to living twice or in two ways ("bis"). Johnson's first sentence thus can be seen both to affirm and deny Martial's portrait of memory's contentment, writing under a kind of erasure an account of life's narrow span as so attenuated that memory alone does not "relieve the vacuities of our being."

Further, if we are "forced" by our lack of presence, our life of gaps, to turn "every moment" to the past and future, then we cannot be said to have experienced life itself in any full or direct sense as we live it. As Johnson says shortly in this essay, the present is "in perpetual motion," and it "leaves us as soon as it arrives, ceases to be present as soon as its presence is well perceived, and is only known to have existed by the effects it leaves behind" (3:223–24). How is this statement, aside from its clarity, different from Derrida's just-mentioned description of consciousness as the trace of an effect, a trace that is caught up in the past and future, which are also characterized by difference and deferral? The here and now, both Johnson and Derrida appear to be telling us, is never really here and now, no matter what our common sense says. The

74

present is known only by the effect of its absence, by its other, by an endless substitution that never restores the always-already-lacking "presence" of the present. Our lives thus may seem to us remarkably like those subatomic particles we can never observe except, in extraordinary circumstances, by the traces they leave behind.

Further, Johnson's reference here to "supplemental satisfactions" would seem to exemplify Derrida's important concept of the unavoidable "supplement," which reveals how something is always lacking in what is presumed already completed.[4] In Johnson's statement, the past and future cannot in any unproblematic way "supplement" the present because they are already involved in the present by virtue of our "recourse every moment" to the "recollection of former passages, or anticipation of events to come." The original phrasing of the folio version is even more emphatic, referring to "former accidents" rather than "former passages," thus suggesting that any illusion of presence we have had should be considered an irregularity, even a mishap in the universal scheme. Johnson sees the need in the mirage of our experience for "an originary supplement," as Derrida puts it, "if this absurd expression may be risked, totally unacceptable as it is within classical logic" (*Grammatology* 313). ("Originary" in fact occurs in Johnson's *Dictionary*, along with "misprision," "narrify," "to privilege" as a verb, and other familiarly strange terms, as Hagstrum has noted.) When we search in the past and future for something to fill up or complete our present void, we necessarily find that those moments are also impure, inscribed in their own "recourse" to some inconclusive supplement. So we are never fully content because "the natural flights of the human mind," as Johnson asserts early on, "are not from pleasure to pleasure, but from hope to hope" (3:10). It is not that the pleasures are totally absent; they are just never fully here—and so we ramble about, always on their trace.

As the editors of the *Yale Edition* observe, this idea of an absence inherent in life, which begins *Rambler* 41, recurs "throughout the *Rambler*" (5:221n.1), and they cite two essays from the beginning of the series (numbers 2 and 5) and two essays from the end (numbers 203 and 207). For James Boyd White the inadequacy of life, the perdurability of desire, is Johnson's "deepest theme" (145). Certainly it is a recurrent idea. The opening essay addresses the hunger of readers who constantly seek out "the allurement of novelty," shifting "the gale of favor" this way and that (3:8; 3:4). The second essay observes how frequently writers have remarked "that the mind of man is never satisfied with the objects immediately before it, but is always breaking away from the present moment, and losing itself in schemes of future felicity" (3:9). The problem with pleasing audiences, according to the third essay, is the difficulty of continually finding something new to say, or at least making the old look new. Immoral fictions, as the fourth essay reveals, are dangerous because we desire any distraction, and those "minds unfurnished with ideas" are "easily susceptible of impressions" (3:12). The fifth essay begins with an idea that has already been declared in the second essay to be so familiar that we ignore it when we see it: "Every man is sufficiently discontented with some circumstances of his present state, to suffer his imagination to range more or less in quest of future happiness" (3:25). In fact, the idea appears in some form in virtually every essay, and it is central in at least twenty-four.[5]

If we consider for the moment that Johnson's conception of the spatial and temporal self may be in some sense deconstructive, we might next look for some obvious consequences of that idea. The problem of choosing, for example, of selecting and evaluating alternatives, is profoundly affected by a deconstructive perspective. It is a problem that apparently fascinated Johnson, for "The Choice of Life," which was of course the working title for *Rasselas*, could have worked as the title for almost any of his productions. How does Johnson characteristically think of choosing? In terms that do seem quite deconstructive: as the finally arbitrary preference for one member of a tragically polarized and irreducible opposition. One of the most familiar instances occurs in *Rasselas*, when Nekayah confirms Imlac's principle, "so often uttered," that "nature sets her gifts on the right hand and on the left" (72). Since "no man can taste the fruits of autumn while he is delighting his scent with the flowers of spring" or "fill his cup from the source and from the mouth of the Nile," we are faced with paralysis or choice. Because "we cannot seize both" alternatives, we always miss the fullness of nature: "as we approach one, we recede from another." Nekayah advises Rasselas to "make your choice and be content," but we notice that Rasselas continues to defer, unable to tell the difference. If "marriage has many pains, but celibacy few pleasures," how should one decide? When Rasselas accuses Nekayah of presenting both options as the "worst," she responds, with a Derridean shrug, "We differ from ourselves just as we differ from each other" (68). The same situation recurs again and again in Johnson's works. The lexicographer repeatedly finds, for example, as Johnson says in the *Dictionary*'s preface, that "choice was to be made without any established principle of selection" (24). Deconstruction, Derrida says, exposes "undecidables . . . that can no longer be included within philosophical (binary) opposition"—"marks" that fail "*ever*" to constitute "a third term" (*Positions* 42–43).

This idea of arbitrary oppositions bound up within each other suffuses the idea of choosing in *The Rambler*. Number 178 for instance says that gratifications are set "at such a distance from each other, that no art or power can bring them together," and it is "impossible to approach one but by receding from the other" (5:173). We must simply determine a "preference" and then "withdraw our eyes and our thoughts at once from that which reason directs us to reject"—or otherwise deconstruct our lives away "in an attempt to make contradictions consistent, to combine opposite qualities" (5:173).

Polyphilus in *Rambler* 19 is one of many characters caught up in just such an interminable analysis, for any man "who balances all the arguments on every side" will find that "reason is forced at last to rest in neutrality," and "the decision devolves into the hands of chance," or stagnation (3:109). As Johnson writes four essays later, any examination sufficiently inclusive will result in our being "held in perpetual suspense between contrary impulses" (3:126). In a deconstructed world, as John Sheriff says, "the search for presence, being, truth is a fool's errand, a quixotic quest" (46). Very early in *The Rambler*, in the second essay, Johnson observes how we are all like "the knight of La Mancha" (3:11)—erring, wandering, ramblers.

To these provisionally deconstructive traits—an extreme skepticism; a vision of consciousness, space, and time in terms of the trace or mirage; a sense of inevitable incompleteness and inadequacy, embodied in the idea of "the supplement"; and a conception of the dyadic and arbitrary nature of choosing—I want to add a final and fundamental trait. Deconstruction is not simply based on a theory of language; its theory seems to be that everything in a certain sense *is* language. As Derrida's most famous saying goes, "There is no outside to the text," or "There is nothing outside of the text" ("il n'y a pas de hors texte" [*Grammatology* 158]).

Does Johnson in any way manifest such a view of language? Does he perceive that language allows no "transparent window on to an established 'reality,'" as Terence Hawkes says (146), and that "nothing is conceivable for us" outside of the language we find ourselves in, as Derrida says (*Grammatology* 13)? Although it is difficult to imagine that Johnson's dictionary is based on Derridean principles (or to imagine such a dictionary at all for that matter), and nearly unthinkable that Johnson would agree there is nothing outside the text with so many stones just a kick away, nevertheless Johnson's philosophy of language may in some significant aspects seem deconstructive.

In fact, in two engaging essays Cyril Knoblauch has already gathered one kind of evidence, in large part from *The Rambler*, for precisely such a linking of deconstruction and Johnson's philosophy of language. Knoblauch shows us how Johnson's writing embodies an "ironic realization of the insufficiency of the Word" ("Composing" 262) and how Johnson perceives that "the statement is doomed to inadequacy, to infinite rewriting," because "something is always left out; something more can always be said" ("Coherence" 237). According to Knoblauch, Johnson's insight into the "rupture" or "divorce" between words and things—the "daughters of earth" and the "sons of heaven" as Johnson calls them—is crucial to his awareness that writing is always about itself and therefore "takes us no nearer the truth" ("Composing" 255). It is thus the Mad Astronomer who most dramatically portrays the human condition in *Rasselas*, doomed to generate "pleasing fictions" and "verbal self-delusion" ("Coherence" 255).

To substantiate Johnson's grasp of the "necessarily tentative and ephemeral" status of writing, Knoblauch refers for example to Johnson's sense of libraries as "monuments to the failure of writing as a cultural enterprise" ("Composing" 244). In *Ramblers* 2 and 106 Johnson observes how "every catalogue of a library" is crowded with forgotten names (3:13), and how "innumerable authors" are "treasured up in magnificent obscurity" (4:201). Knoblauch also cites *Idler* 65 in which Johnson refers to Thomas Baker, who "left his manuscripts buried in a library, because that was imperfect which could not be perfected" (2:204), a sad testimony to the impotent insularity of language. "Definition," Knoblauch observes Johnson saying in *Rambler* 125, "is not the province of man" (4:300), and therefore Johnson's preface "effectively sabotages the achievement of the *Dictionary* and mocks explicitly . . . the inadequacy of the author" ("Coherence" 246). "No dictionary of a living tongue," Johnson says, "ever can be perfect, since while it is hastening to publication, some words are budding, and some falling away" (Preface 245). Surrendering to the confusion of usage, Johnson comes to see the arbitrariness, the open-endedness, of a system that "is self-contained and self-generating, a text upon a text" ("Coherence" 241); he comes to acknowledge "the irretrievable loss of the once vital unity between language and a universe both beyond and within language" ("Coherence" 242).

If Johnson does perhaps adopt a skeptical attitude toward consciousness, space, time, completeness, choosing, and language—an attitude that can be meaningfully juxtaposed to Derrida and deconstruction—then what intellectual context allows Johnson to evolve this outlook? If poststructuralism starts from Saussure's conception of the sign, what linguistic theory grounds Johnson's thinking? What context, if any, helps account for Johnson's "deconstruction," and does that context further align Johnson with modern-day poststructuralists or does it perhaps help to distinguish

Johnson's thought? In other words, having briefly considered Johnson in terms of our own time, I would like now to consider these
same notions in terms of his age.

It is widely agreed that Johnson receives an essentially Lockean view of language. Robert DeMaria, writing about the *Dictionary*,
reflects the consensus view of this inheritance when he says that
Johnson sees language as "the only adequate vehicle and receptacle
of knowledge" ("Theory" 159). Although Johnson must recognize
with Locke and others that no "artificial organization of language
can ever be instituted over the existing power of usage," he believes
that "language would be better if it were organized on strictly logical
principles," ideally like the "unequivocal symbolism of mathematics" ("Theory" 160). This desire, DeMaria notes, places Johnson
in the company of a variety of language reformers—he mentions
Ephraim Chambers, Comenius, Bishop Wilkins, and Vives—who
sought to conform language more effectively to knowledge, and
moreover to seek knowledge by way of words. DeMaria draws
attention especially to Chambers' *Cyclopedia*, the work Johnson said
shaped his prose style (Boswell 1:218–19).

Chambers' idea of language appears today more like something Jorge Luis Borges would have imagined than the considered
outlook of a respected lexicographer. Just as Borges' library of Babel
held all possible books and thus all possible knowledge, Chambers
makes the even more outrageous assertion that the "whole compass
of words, in all their cases," is "equivalent to the whole system
of possible science" (1:xi). Like many radical language reformers,
Chambers envisions a distant past, probably in Egypt, "when
words were more complex and obscure than now; and mystic sym-
bols and hieroglyphics obtained; so that an explication of their
marks or words might amount to a revelation of their whole inner
philosophy" (1:xvi).

Thus when DeMaria says that Johnson inherits Chambers'
commitment to "a basically Lockean view of the relations between
language and knowledge" (162), it is unclear what he means.
Locke's great *Essay*, as Hans Aarsleff has shown, set out to dismantle just the sort of Adamic and philosophical conceptions of language that Chambers seems to endorse.[6] To be sure, Locke shares

the desire of Chambers and many others to make language conform to knowledge and reality, but Locke seems to recognize the impossibility of this desire. While he acknowledges that "*God*, having designed Man for a sensible Creature . . . furnished him also with language" (402), Locke does not believe we should attempt to recreate some powerful Adamic tongue, because Adam had the same liberty as any other man "to make complex Ideas of mixed Modes, by no other Pattern, but by his own Thoughts" and to try to conform "his Ideas of Substances to Things" (470). We may strive to repair the ruins of Babel by attempting "to know Things as they are" and to "speak of things really existing" (456). However,

> it is evident the mind knows not things immediately but only by the intervention of the ideas it has of them. Our knowledge, therefore, is real only so far as there is a *conformity* between our ideas and the reality of things. But what shall be here the criterion? How shall the mind, when it perceives nothing but its own ideas, know that they agree with things themselves? (563)

Locke thus divorces words from things by denying our ability to know when words conform to things. Moreover he is deeply skeptical of any order we might perceive in "things themselves." He has seen with his own eyes the issue of a cat mated with a rat; he has read of a creature "with a Man's Head and Hog's Body" and of women impregnated by monkeys; he knows from chemists, especially from his friend Boyle, that different samples of gold do not behave in exactly the same way.[7]

These and other examples call into question for Locke the validity of natural "kinds" or "sorts," and he concludes that "the boundaries of the Species, whereby Men set them, are made by Men" (462). More abstract terms, such as "justice" or "equality," would appear to be hopelessly unanchored, being "assemblages of Ideas put together at the pleasure of the Mind, pursuing its own ends of Discourse, and suited to its own Notions" (478). Thus Locke's desire for some connection between words, ideas, and things is rendered untenable by the arbitrariness of language, the ambiguity of nature, and the multiplicity of things.

According to Art Berman, who is presenting a surprisingly common view, Locke naively believes that "language is partitioned like the external array of objects themselves" (16); "his theory of language is a 'correspondence' or 'referential' theory" (15).[8] But Locke's view is by no means so simple or innocent (his biology, admittedly, may be faulty by our standards). For Locke, ideas in any speaker stand in an uncertain relationship to the arbitrary conventions of language and the unbounded appearances of reality. Thus Locke chooses as the *Essay*'s motto these appropriate lines from Ecclesiastes: "As thou knowest not what is the way of the Spirit, nor how the bones do grow in the Womb of her that is with Child: even so thou knowest not the works of God, who maketh all things." His essay on human understanding is in truth a map of misunderstanding, urging caution, care, and tolerance.

To expand the context Johnson inhabits it may be useful to note that both George Campbell and Hugh Blair, arguably the two most significant eighteenth-century rhetoricians, reflect views close to Locke's. Like Locke, Blair says that language "must have a Divine original" (101), and therefore "throughout the radical words of all Languages, there may be traced some degree of correspondence with the object signified" (103). Yet Blair also negates this implication of an Adamic tongue by asserting that words are "arbitrary, or instituted, not natural signs of ideas" (106). Campbell's position is similar. The connection between "words and things," he says, "hath not its foundation in the nature of things, but in the conventions of man" (258). As in algebra and mathematics, Campbell says, we need not form an exact idea of "the quantities and sums signified" to draw "accurate and convincing" conclusions (264, 265). In "some instances," in fact, such exactitude "is even impossible" (264); but "by the regular structure of a language, this connexion among the signs is conceived as analogous to that which subsisteth among their archetypes" (260). We do not know those archetypes, words being arbitrarily related to things, but we can imagine we know them, and the "effect upon the mind is much the same" (258).

Although Johnson wrote both the "Plan" and preface for the *Dictionary* before Campbell and Blair's major works appeared in print, he exhibits the same sort of yearning for presence, origins,

82

meaning, coherence that we see in Locke, Blair, and Campbell, and that appears to be analogous to the logocentric desire that Derrida again and again uncovers and interrogates. After promising in the "Plan" that English will "be laid down, distinct in its minutest subdivisions, and resolved into its elemental principles," Johnson goes on to ask, "And who upon this survey can forbear to wish, that these fundamental atoms of our speech might obtain the firmness and immutability of the primogenial and constitutuent particles of matter?" (12). In *Idler* 88 Johnson places such desires for "a real character" in the same class as efforts to create a "universal medicine" and a "perpetual motion machine" (2:273), and his own wish for an immutable speech in the "Plan" is dismissed just as decisively: "Language is the work of man," Johnson writes, "from whom permanence and stability cannot be derived" (12).

But the desire for origins, essence, presence, and truth, despite our recognition of the impossibility of its fulfillment, will continue to recur. When Johnson comes to write the *Dictionary's* preface, this desire to establish a "real" language, already dismissed in the "Plan," is reconstituted into an earlier intention. Johnson asserts that at the outset of his project he had planned to search "into the original of words" and then to "show likewise my attention to things; to pierce deep into every science, to inquire the nature of every substance of which I inserted the name, to limit every idea by a definition strictly logical" (42–43). He implies here he had planned to employ both the Adamic and the scientific approaches to language reform. Johnson's recurring desire for a "real" language that he knows must be denied thus drives him to recreate an original intention that according to his "Plan" never really existed except as an impossible longing, dismissed from the start. Such, Johnson says, are "the dreams of a poet, doomed to wake a lexicographer" (Preface 43), for words are not only the "arbitrary representation of sounds by letters" (25) but are even "variable by the caprice of everyone that speaks," with some words "hourly shifting their relations" (35). Making a dictionary, Johnson exclaims in frustration, is like accurately delineating "a grove, in the agitation of a storm," by examining "its picture in the water" (35).

Yet despite his apparent awareness of something like the myth of logocentrism, Johnson many years later, in 1783, after achieving perhaps the greatest individual delineation of the fluid grove of language, is still dreaming of an original, pure tongue. He tells John Walker that "language must have come by inspiration," because "a thousand, nay, a million children could not invent a language" (Boswell 4:207). Man could no more create a language without the inspiration of a divine Logos, Johnson says, "than cows or hogs would think of such a faculty." To Walker's query whether "there are any perfect synonymies in any language," Johnson responds, "Originally there were not; but by using words negligently, or in poetry, one word comes to be confounded with another." Years earlier, ignoring the Biblical implications, Johnson had offered in the "Plan" another view of the origin and decay of language, which "did not descend to us in a state of uniformity and perfection, but was produced by necessity, and enlarged by accident, and is therefore, composed of dissimilar parts, thrown together by negligence, by affectation, by learning or by ignorance" (11).

Johnson's view of langauge, it appears, involves the recurrent deconstruction of a powerfully tempting and always returning myth of a pristine origin. Locke, Blair, Campbell, and Johnson thus appear to inherit the reformers' desire for a more "real" language, yet they also reluctantly recognize that actual language is arbitrary, unconventional, divorced from things. Are they all in this sense deconstructionists? John Ellis, among others, asserts that the logocentric error is "a problem with which we were all familiar long before Derrida" (37), and it does appear that Johnson and others recognized in some sense that their longing for "a full speech that was fully *present*," "an originary speech" (*Grammatology* 8), could not be satisfied.[9]

Thus this break between words and things, leading to calls for a more "mathematical," orderly, science-based language on the one hand (as in the work of Isaac Watts and William Duncan), and to a disturbing epistemological skepticism on the other (as in Berkeley and Hume), is already present in Locke, along with the alternative consequences. But Locke's idea of the gap between words and things, and the space he opens for Johnson and others to think about language and knowledge, can in fact be usefully distinguished from Derrida's abyss. A brief return to Knoblauch will suggest how we might begin to make such a distinction.

Derrida sees two views of language, polar opposites: the logo-centric view versus the vision that strives to expose logocentrism and the illusion of presence. Knoblauch similarly appears to think in binary terms. On the one hand there is an Adamistic harmony of words and things, enabling the linguistic "power of magic," "of miracles and prophecies and prayer" ("Coherence" 257). And on the other hand there are "the habits of mind which we still share with Johnson's era," which "fractured human experience" into "the world of sense and the world of mind," revealing "a divorce be-tween things . . . and words" ("Coherence" 237). Knoblauch's cited source, however, is not Derrida but Foucault. Although Derrida and Foucault both may be called poststructuralists, their positions are significantly different. As Peter Flaherty puts it,

> While Derrida feels that the text must be relentlessly "deconstructed," so that its network of "traces" can be better exposed as trapped within the "prison-house" of logocentrism, Foucault takes the position that a text can be best read against its context, that is, as part of a larger set of discursive practices that inform the *episteme* of its specific spatio-temporal configuration. (165)

Foucault, perhaps less controlled by a binary schema, discusses a third age between the Renaissance and modern orientations, a "classical" period dating from the seventeenth to the nineteenth centuries. In this *episteme*, Foucault says, the relationship between words and things is seen as one of "representation." Although language is no longer considered to be inextricably linked to the real world, language nonetheless may stand for the world, allowing us to assemble, classify, analyze, criticize—in other words, make sense. In this period, language, properly used, is not assumed to be only about itself, with "nothing to say but itself" (Foucault 300).

Roy Harris's three orientations toward language—surroga-tionalism, instrumentalism, and contractualism—correspond roughly to Foucault's three ages, although Harris offers a more optimistic view of modern writing. The work of Hans Aarsleff and Murray Cohen, among others, also supports the idea that Johnson's age by and large viewed language in representational terms, as a capable instrument for examining "things," but by no means naturally or necessarily connected to or in harmony with them. Most of the time in almost every profession, the habits of mind of this in-between age are in truth the ones we still share with Johnson's era.

If we look more closely at Knoblauch's examples, mentioned above, we may see that Johnson consistently seems most interested in how the failure of writing results from human folly or ignorance, and not vice-versa. The limitations of language, when they figure in Johnson's thinking, are equally likely to be seen as a benefit or liability. To return to the second *Rambler* for instance, Johnson's reference to libraries and their catalogues crowded with forgotten names can be seen as part of a strategic effort to remind any author (including himself) how other writers "no less enterprising or confident than himself, equally pleased with their productions, equally caressed by their patrons, and flattered by their friends" might nevertheless fail (3:13). It would be difficult to argue that Johnson sees the failure of such self-confident, self-pleased, patron-pampered and friend-flattered authors as necessarily a bad thing, or that he implicitly attributes such failure to the nature of language. Further, Johnson does not imply the certainty of failure, and he acknowledges that expectations—sometimes even great ones—are necessary preconditions for success. The essay ends in a precarious balancing of hope and resignation, with the writer (and any one by implication) aware that if he should succeed, "he is indebted to other causes besides his industry, his learning, or his wit" (3:14).

It seems clear enough that whatever might help us succeed ("other causes"), what hinders us is not language itself. The problem instead is the psychology of the reader. As Johnson says in the second *Rambler*, "What is new is opposed, because most are unwilling to be taught; and what is known is rejected, because it is not sufficiently considered, that men more frequently require to be reminded than informed" (3:14). This statement, echoed throughout Johnson's canon, seems to explain why reminding, the more important endeavor (or more frequently required) is unsuccessful. But it actually evades that promise, and thereby exemplifies Johnson's point. The writer who does sufficiently consider that readers need more often to be reminded will take into account the essay's opening principle, "that the mind of man is never satisfied with the objects immediately before it" and is "always breaking away" for some as yet unknown "felicity" (3:9). Johnson thus removes what we already know from his articulation of why writers fail to recommend what we already know. Writers fail (as we already [impatiently] know) because we are impatient with what we already know.

Johnson also embodies the principle that we need more frequently to be reminded by immediately reminding us in the third essay of what we have just learned in the second essay, formally stating "the task of an author" in these same terms of "new" versus "known." Teaching "what is not known" appears to be a simple matter of vision, letting "new light in upon the mind," opening "new scenes to the prospect" (3:15). But recommending "known truths" is presented in terms of a seduction or temptation, as the author must "vary the dress and situation of common objects, so as to give them fresh grace and more powerful attractions." The author must "tempt" his audience "to return, and take a second view" by spreading "such flowers over the region" that the familiar seems new. For an author to succeed, readers "must not only confess their ignorance, but, what is still less pleasing, must allow that he from whom they are to learn is more knowing than themselves" (3:15). This allowance must be particularly irksome when readers are being informed of something they already know. Thus, ironically, it seems we are least receptive to what we most need to hear ("men more frequently require to be reminded than informed"). This irony is hardly the fault of language; in fact, language can entice us to overcome this resistance.

The motto for *Rambler* 106, another essay cited by Knoblauch, might well seem to be a condensation of the allegory in *Rambler* 3, published exactly one year earlier. "Time obliterates the fictions of opinion," Johnson translates from Cicero, "and confirms the decisions of nature" (4:199). Again Johnson turns to libraries for the most striking evidence of "the vanity of human hopes." He displays an interest in "the fragile character of writing as it exists in time," as Knoblauch says, but this "historical erosion" turns out for Johnson to be a strength, more of a factor in the present success of writing than its failure. This point can be seen most cogently in Johnson's first comment on those works "treasured up in magnificent obscurity" (4:201). Most authors are forgotten, we read, "because they never deserved to be remembered" (4:201). Although some scholars may "bewail the loss of ancient writers whose characters have survived their works," we should likely find if their works were miraculously retrieved "only the Granvilles, Montagues, Stepneys, and Sheffields of their time." Other writers, "whom it were unjust to number with this despicable class," have limited their duration by writing on "temporary subjects," no longer of interest or significance (4:201, 202). Likewise, some "controvertists" have dealt with questions that are quickly decided or impossible to decide, and hence they have been deservedly forgotten—a consequence that is hardly the fault of writing itself (4:203). Even the announcements of spectacular scientific discoveries often fade away, Johnson says, because the resourcefulness of language and human effort allows clearer and more concise explanations naturally to follow. Elsewhere Johnson reiterates that the "most esteemed" works have survived, "so that having the originals, we may without much regret have lost imitations" (2:206). Some "single passages" may now be obscure, but the "general tendency of every piece may be known." Moreover, Johnson asserts, "the most useful truths are always universal, and unconnected with accidents and customs" (2:206). Finally, if every work from antiquity had survived, "almost every subject would have been fixed by a precedent from which few would have ventured to depart." As we have seen, Johnson was acutely aware of how the precedent of *The Spectator* stood in the way of essayists coming after. One can deal with only a limited number of precursors.

One of Knoblauch's most affecting examples is Johnson's "sad comment" on Thomas Baker, who after many years of writing "left his manuscripts buried in a library, because that was imperfect which could not be perfected" ("Composing" 246). Johnson's comment certainly appears at first glance to illustrate his sense of the open-ended, necessarily insufficient nature of writing. But looking closer we see that Baker failed not because of the "depleted" status of language but because of an even more serious depletion: he died. Prescribing for himself "such a degree of exactness as human diligence can scarcely attain," Baker illustrates once more the vanity of human wishes rather than the endless deferral of meaning. After all, Anthony Wood had already done for Oxford what Baker hoped to do for Cambridge, and as the Yale editors point out Baker did complete some forty-two volumes (*Idler* 2:204n.1). In fact, Johnson's closing remarks seem to take for granted the adequacy of language for human purposes if we lower our standards to a reasonable, human level.

> Let it always be remembered that life is short, that knowledge is endless, and that many doubts deserve not to be cleared. Let those whom nature and study have qualified to teach mankind, tell us what they have learned while they are yet able to tell it. (2:204)

This point is similar to Johnson's reflection in *Rambler* 23 that the reader who "accommodates his mind to the author's design" is "often contented without pleasure, and pleased without perfection" (3:127). Writing may adequately serve worthy purposes even when obviously faulty.

The "debasement of rhetoric," the awareness that "all writing is necessarily tentative and emphemeral," is also supposedly seen in Johnson's statement in *Rambler* 125 that "definition is . . . not the province of man" (4:300). But the problem with definition in this essay is not so much the impotence of language but the mutability of "things modified by human understandings" (4:300). Nature is too enormous and complex and art is "too inconstant and uncertain" to be "reduced to any determinate idea." Of course, whether language is inadequate, or nature too complex, or art too uncertain, the effect is arguably the same: we remain in ignorance. But the significance of this distinction is pointed up by the rest of Johnson's essay. Comedy, Johnson tells us, "not being limited by nature, cannot be comprised in precept" (4:301). Some "new genius" can always expand and alter the rules of a genre, including "comedy." This adaptability is hardly tragic. Moreover, language allows us to offer a precept that may accurately describe "comedy" at a particular time, which is precisely what Johnson proposes in this essay, giving us a more expansive and accurate definition based on "effects upon the mind" (4:301) rather than formal features.

Johnson complains that "no dictionary of a living tongue can ever be perfect," but the lexicographer's problem—which Johnson plays for all the pathetic appeal he can—is the consequence of a "living" language's ability to adapt and renew itself (and admittedly to decay and fragment if not attended). Perhaps Johnson's most revealing statement about language occurs in this consideration of the lowly question of orthography:

> This recommendation of steadiness and uniformity does not proceed from an opinion that particular combinations of letters have much influence on human happiness; or that truth may not be successfully taught by modes of spelling fanciful and erroneous: I am not yet so lost in lexicography, as to forget that words are the daughters of earth and that things are the sons of heaven. (*Works* 5:27)

This depiction of words as "the daughters of earth" and things as "the sons of heaven" cannot fairly be used to indicate Johnson's awareness of a profoundly disabling gap between words and things. Instead, Johnson is alluding to Genesis 6:2, where "the sons of God" marry "the daughters of earth." As in all marriages, words and things are separate and different; they may be married or divorced; their conjunction may or may not produce some legitimate offspring. If Johnson wants us to take the denial that "particular combinations of letters have much influence upon human happiness" as the gloomy endorsement of language's "illusion sustained by artifice," it is only so he can affectingly stand this inference on its head, as the rhetorical potency of language appears immediately in its ability to convey "truth" even in "fanciful and erroneous" forms.

Thus, reexamining Knoblauch's supporting evidence suggests that writing in Johnson's view is actually a resilient, durable medium, generally adequate for persuasive human needs. Even apparent defects of language sometimes become productive strengths, as the loss of poor and derivative works opens a space for modern attempts. Johnson is aware of a natural entropy, a slippage, in writing, but the deficiencies of readers and writers account more for the (often fortuitous) failure of writing than the nature of language itself. Despite Johnson's apparent grasp of much involved in deconstruction, this difference in his view of language is crucial. The Derridean maxim, "There is nothing outside the text," takes on a profoundly different meaning in a Johnsonian context, and by investigating this difference I hope to demarcate further the space between Johnson and Derrida.

"Wide and Continued Vacuity"

According to Hester Thrale, the idea of nothingness, specifically of "the vacuity of life," "had at some early period become by repeated impressions" Johnson's "favourite hypothesis" (Hill 1:251). Thrale's recognition of the importance of this idea for Johnson (which was not adequately perceived by Boswell) is often cited, but to my knowledge the context of her statement has not been considered.[10] By no means does Thrale intend to imply the endpoint of Johnson's reasonings, "wherever they might begin," constitutes a profound, or even a sensible insight. Instead her remarks, following a passage in which Johnson is shown to have sided always with the husband in any marital dispute, no matter what the facts, furthers her implication that Johnson's thinking, despite his amazing abilities, is in fundamental ways seriously flawed. While "other philsophers" identify "various and contradictory causes," Johnson, Thrale says, chronically employs one explanation for everything (just as he takes a one-sided view of marital differences): "All was done to fill up the time, upon his principle" (Hill 1:251). In fact, Thrale's image of Johnson's "repeated impressions" forming a "favourite hypothesis" is especially discrediting in the context of eighteenth-century Lockean psychology. It is "a sort of madness," Locke

91

says, when certain paths of thought, by frequent "treading," become "worn into a smooth path, and the Motion in it becomes easy and as it were Natural" (396). Although Thrale's famous reference to Johnson's padlock is more sensational, her discussion of his universally applicable principle of explanation depicts more explicitly an obsessional Johnson, enchained by an unreasonable association of ideas.

I point out how Hester Thrale undermines Johnson's "favourite hypothesis" by linking it to his fixated personality because some modern readers have also tended similarly to dismiss or downplay this crucial idea. Arieh Sachs finds that "in terms of Johnson the 'public figure' such passages [on the vacuity of life] are the uninteresting output of a ponderous writer and conversationalist, whose claim to permanence . . . lies much more in his acute literary criticism" (19). It is only, Sachs says, "in the context of the anguished man 'shut in his den,' fully experiencing the 'vacuity of life'" that "such passages become fascinating moral literature." Johnson's "elaborate (and highly original) rethinking of the Christian and Humanist heritage" is for Sachs a kind of curiosity, interesting only "in terms of Johnson's particular being, that is, of his biography" (10). Sachs underscores the peculiarity of Johnson's outlook as well, asserting that his "concept of the 'vacuity of life' was abstracted from an experience of mental blankness and stagnation that had nothing general or formal about it" (11). Robert Voitle similarly connects the vacuity theme to "the man himself," even though the distinction between "moral doctrines" and man is admittedly tenuous in the case of "basic convictions" (137). J. P. Hardy likewise finds Johnson's idea that the vacuity of life is "a strong proof" of the soul's celestial nature nothing more than a shallow and "convenient rationalization" (87), soothing his troubled mind.

These critics miss a crucial fact. For Johnson, the gap, the space, the aporia, the no-thing, the trace of what is absent, is real—that is, it is *really* not there. What I mean by this assertion may be clarified by *Rambler* 8. The first paragraph of this essay says that "the most active and industrious of mankind" would find, upon careful reflection, how very few of his actions left "any permanent or visible effects," and how astonishingly many "chasms . . . of wide and continued vacuity, how many interstitial spaces unfilled," actually composed his life. The powerful forces drawing our time and attention away from piety in the prior essay, *Rambler 7*, are now shown to be in truth almost nonexistent. Johnson shortly acknowledges in *Rambler 8* that probably we are always thinking, but "the common occasions of our present condition require but a small part of that incessant cogitation" (3:42). In suggesting that "incessant cogitation" does not contradict a "wide and continued vacuity" of consciousness, Johnson is entering the widespread discussion of identity that followed upon Locke's refutation of Descartes' claim that "the soul always thinks" (cited in *Idler* 2:76).[11] Johnson's more extensive consideration of this question in *Idler* 24 may help us understand the context of *Rambler* 8, some eight years earlier.

Those who say that the soul always thinks, Johnson says in *Idler* 24, forget that we spend much time in sleep "without the least remembrance of any thoughts which then passed in our minds" (2:76). Those who conclude therefore that the soul sometimes does not think forget that "we every day do something which we forget when it is done, and know to have been done only by consequence." Johnson disdains, however, such a deconstructive conclusion as this: "To discover only that the arguments on both sides are defective, and to throw back the tenet into its former uncertainty, is the sport of wanton or malevolent scepticism, delighting to see the sons of philosophy at work upon a task which can never be completed" (2:77). So he avoids such a dissemination of the problem by asserting, conditionally, "If it be impossible to think without materials, there must necessarily be minds that do not always think"—for example, "the glutton between his meals," "the sportsman in a rainy month," "the annuitant between the days of quarterly payment," "the politician when the mails are detained." Such a person, "in torpid insensibility," just like someone oblivious to the spring, "wants nothing of a carcase but putrefaction" (2:77).

Rambler 8 is less brutal, but the implications of our temporal vacuity, "the interstitial spaces unfilled" even in "the most tumultuous hurries of business, and the most eager vehemence of persuit" (3:41), are nonetheless disturbing. We may always think, but if the object of our thoughts is ephemeral then it is as if we had not—as if we existed mostly within those synapses of consciousness that Locke terms "duration," which is "the distance between any parts of that succession, or between the appearance of any two ideas in our minds" (182). Johnson's assertion in *Rambler* 2 that the mind is "always breaking away from the present moment, and losing itself" becomes particularly ominous against this Lockean background.

In the second paragraph of *Rambler* 8, Johnson compares this vacuity of time to its spatial corollary. Certain "modern philosophers," Johnson says, claim "that not only the great globes of matter are thinly scattered thro' the universe, but the hardest bodies are so porous, that, if all matter were compressed to perfect solidity, it might be contained in a cube of a few feet" (3:41). With our radio telescopes and electron microscopes, we might want to assume that we are uniquely cognizant of the vast emptiness within galaxies or atoms, but Johnson's sense of the relative emptiness of space and the collapsibility of matter at least rivals our own. Johnson, in fact, was not alone in this outlook within his own century. Henry Pemberton, for instance, goes even further, speculating in 1728 that "all the known bodies in the universe" might be "reduced to a globe of one inch" (3). Without any concept of black holes or singularities, the Big Bang or the big crunch, but certainly anticipating their basis, Johnson and many of his contemporaries had concluded, in the words of Isaac Watts, whose work Johnson admired, that "a Vacuum or Void space" virtually comprised the universe. According to Watts in 1742, "every one agrees to it" (2). In other words, the gap, the space, the aporia, is not merely a linguistic or psychological effect but is grounded in physical reality and its psychological effects.

This crucial difference in nothing, so to speak, between Derrida and Johnson, leads me to the most important gap between them. Very simply, Johnson believes. He believes, in deconstructive terms, in a "transcendent signifier" that he calls "providence," "the celestial original," "the divine will," "the author of our being," "the Supreme Benefactor," "the Master," "that being, to whom we are accountable for our thoughts and actions," and, rarely, "God." This belief, it has often been agreed, was by no means easily won.

Studies of the troubled nature of Johnson's faith have tended perhaps to focus on the "very scanty record" of his private journals, as Nicholas Hudson asserts. Johnson's published statements suggest he "gleaned considerable confidence from the knowledge that he was carrying on the convictions and arguments of a venerable tradition of Christian orthodoxy" (2). Even so, Johnson's is a faith that in private and in print appears somehow to have been built out of an acute sense of absence and skepticism. Of Hume's most devastating dismantling of miracles, causality, and ultimately God, Johnson said that "everything which Hume advanced against Christianity had passed through my mind long before he wrote" (Boswell 1:444). If Johnson really means this and knows what he is talking about, then how does Johnson's faith get past Hume's attack?

According to Chester Chapin, it does not: Johnson simply avoids confronting Hume's argument (84–91). Charles Pierce attributes this avoidance to Johnson's suppressed recognition that he could not refute Hume (46–52). Hume's attack on miracles is formidable. John Price describes Hume's strategy this way:

> By temporarily assuming the alleged "truth" of the reasoning which links testimony, miracles, and the Christian religion, Hume was later able to destroy the logic of that "truth" by carrying the logical implications of the propositions concerned to their ultimate limit. Once the "logic" of those propositions is pushed as far as it will go, the inherent contradictions, Hume believes, will be seen. The irony is apparent: what better way to undermine an opponent that to use his own argument against him? (25)

Although this strategy might be seen within the dialectical tradition as an instance of the *reductio ad impossible*, from our perspective it sounds strikingly deconstructive. (Price, writing in 1965, can hardly be accused of attempting to make Hume sound poststructural). As Kevin Hart observes, "Hume's tacit acceptance of a text's prevailing logic in order to uncover its inherent contradictions is remarkably similar to Derrida's own strategy as stated in *Of Grammatology*" (160).

Hume's strategy and his unbelief can thus be placed alongside deconstruction and its consequent atheology, as many readers have perceived it. Carl Raschke for example calls deconstruction "the dance of death upon the tomb of God," an extension of Nietzsche's celebration (28). Eugene Goodheart considers deconstruction to be an "anti-theological skepticism" (13), and Herbert Schneidau calls it "a swipe at Christianity from *arché* to *teloŝ*" (14). Umberto Eco, Mark Taylor, Gayatri Spivak, Eric Gould, Mikel Dufrenne, Peter Kemp, and others argue that deconstruction's effects have been countertheological and atheistic.

But is this connection between deconstruction and the silencing of theology and faith a necessary one? Does faith in deconstruction preclude faith in anything else? Or, returning to Johnsonian terms, must we ignore Hume to believe? Donald Siebert has persuasively argued that "Johnson by no means blindly rejected Hume's reasoning" but rather "found much of Hume's inquiry stimulating and useful—a kind of thinking to be reckoned with, certainly, not rejected out of hand" (543, 544). We return to this question: If Johnson not only understood but anticipated and confronted Hume's position, then how did he create his faith after (Hume's) deconstruction?

Not everyone in fact agrees that after deconstruction there is no room left for faith. A growing number of thinkers are asserting that deconstruction clears a space for faith. Herbert Schneidau explains how our "sudden revelations of meaninglessness or arbitrariness" leave us "decentered," alienated from ourselves, "acutely conscious of the fictionality of things"—in short, at "the pre-condition of insight" (48–49). Our sense of insufficiency and absence thereby may become "a *felix culpa*, good news for modern man of a somewhat unlikely kind" (49). Douglas Atkins argues that deconstruction allows for "the dehellenization of theology," reinserting mystery and freedom into faith, "notably the *freedom* to make" (47). Likewise, Thomas Walsh says deconstruction may be understood as a prelude to a return of theology, even ontotheology: "that rough beast, its hour come round at last, slouching toward

Bethlehem, Paris, or New Haven to be born" (115). John Dominic Crossan believes "what Derrida is saying leads straight into a contemporary retrieval of negative theology," "a theology articulating itself by a philosophy of absence" (11). Robert Magliola finds that deconstruction actually releases a "differential theology" that is strangely enough "disciplined and even 'conservative'" (x). Kevin Hart concludes that adding "the Derridean problematic to theology" provides for mysticism and faith, leading to a "general negative theology." This theology "places the proper name in question, and then provides us with an account of the only possible way in which a theology can resist the illusions of metaphysics" (269).[12]

Although Gayatri Spivak, one of Derrida's most influential translators and interpreters, insists that deconstruction is not "mystical" or "theological" (*Grammatology* lxxviii), Derrida's own statements are by no means so determinate. For one thing, Derrida explicitly recognizes that "the detours, phrases, and syntax that I shall often have to resort to will resemble—will sometimes be practically indiscernible from—those of negative theology" (*Speech* 134). The difference between his project and theology's *via negativa*, Derrida says, is "differance," which is "not theological, not even in the most negative order of negative theology." This distinction does not however disable theology in its positive or negative modes, for it is Derrida's nothing, differance, that also "opens up the very space in which ontotheology—philosophy—produces its system and its history" (*Speech* 134, 135). More mystically, Derrida writes that "the death of God will ensure our salvation because the death of God alone can reawaken the divine" and that "the divine has been ruined by God" (*Writing* 184, 243). In other words, deconstruction opens up the space for positive ontotheology to be written, which is of course immediately subject to an opposing negative theology, removing the "God" we have written and leaving the divine to be reinscribed and again "ruined." Somehow the enabling "differance," Derrida maintains, is both inside and outside this space, as it "encompasses and irrevocably surpasses ontotheology and philosophy" (*Speech* 135). Derrida does assert that "the negative movement of the discourse on God is only a phase of positive ontotheology" because both posit a "superessentiality" (*Writing*

97

337n.37, 271). But this statement must be true only to the same extent that deconstruction is itself only a phase of logocentrism. As Derrida puts it:

> The movements of deconstruction do not destroy structures from the outside. They are not possible and effective, nor can they take accurate aim, except by inhabiting those structures. Inhabiting them *in a certain way*, because one always inhabits, and all the more when one does not suspect it. Operating necessarily from the inside, borrowing all the strategic and economic resources of subversion from the old structure . . . deconstruction always in a certain way falls prey to its own work. (*Grammatology* 24)

Just as negative theology can speak only by inhabiting and subverting positive theology, so can deconstruction work only by inhabiting logocentric structures. There is no outside, only differance, gap, space, void. Deconstruction imagines that a discourse is logically consistent in order to show it is not. Negative theology imagines that a discourse articulates "God" in order to show it does not.

Far from being antithetical to deconstruction, theology seems in Derrida's economy to function as deconstruction. "One can argue," Derrida says, "that these original, heterogenous elements of Judaism and Christianity were never completely eradicated by Western metaphysics. They perdure throughout the centuries, threatening and unsettling the assured 'identities' of Western philosophy" ("Deconstruction" 117). Christian theology is not the object of deconstruction, Kevin Hart says, but is part of the process of deconstruction—"in some of its elements at least" (93). In short, it seems plausible that negative theology is to positive, as Judeo-Christian theology is to Western metaphysics.

My point is this: deconstruction—Humean or Derridean—does not require atheism. On the contrary, "deconstruction always in a certain way falls prey to its own work," and discourses that expose God's absence are as vulnerable as those that announce God's presence. We are left, deconstruction tells us, with an absent Presence or a present Absence. For that reason, in announcing his project Derrida desired to "get to a point at which he does not know where he is going" ("Structure" 267), to see clearly where we are (not). This rambling condition is the focus of Johnson's wandering attention and the moving ground his wondering faith traverses.

"I Cannot But Consider"

Johnson creates his traditional faith *ex nihilo*, in a sense. He gets beyond that "endless clearing or curing of the ground now being called 'deconstruction,'" in Harold Bloom's words (*Poetry* 396), by enacting a faith based finally on nothing, on the absence of something (everything) for which we yearn. This absence is not for Johnson an effect of language, an effect of our being within language, but is symptomatic of a more profound and real nothingness outside "the text." Crucial to Johnson's response to this absence is a way of looking at life that I will call "the cycle of desire." This movement begins with our apprehension of the insufficiency, the abyss even, of the present moment. Faith begins when we notice nothing in a certain way. The opening sentence of *Rambler* 41, which exposes our absence from time and space, is followed immediately by a declaration of the significance of this absence, adumbrating in two sentences the beginning and end of Johnson's philosophy of life, or his cycle of desire: "I cannot but consider this necessity of searching on every side for matter on which the attention may be employed, as a strong proof of the superior and celestial nature of the soul of man" (3:221–22). What is there between the recognition of an absence and the creation of faith that drives Johnson inescapably? Why is it (aside from anxiety and fear) that he "cannot but consider" this lack as the sign of a transcendent present?

To answer these questions let us return here to the sequential analysis of the series and follow the idea of the insufficiency of the present as it shapes Johnson's presentation as well as his "systematical" philosophy.[13] If the proposition beginning *Rambler* 5 is not crucial to something Johnson is trying to get across, then clearly he is obsessed with the idea, as Mrs. Piozzi suggested, or he lacks creativity, as Boswell indicated, or both, for the second essay already has begun by observing how very frequently this same notion has been remarked. As the opening of *Rambler* 5 puts it:

on Spring

> Every man is sufficiently discontented with some circumstances of his present state, to suffer his imagination to range more or less in quest of future happiness, and to fix upon some point of time, in which, by the removal of the inconvenience which now perplexes him, or acquisition of the advantage which he at present wants, he shall find the condition of his life very much improved. (3:25)

The implication that this discontent may be our own fault, which is a repetition from the second essay ("the mind of man is never satisfied with the objects before it," forgetting "the proper use of time now in our power"), is further pursued in *Rambler* 5.

Rambler 5, in telling the story of the man who referred all his hopes to the coming of the next spring, may seem at first to argue forcefully that the vacuity of life is at least in part a matter of perception. Instead of losing oneself in dreams of spring or some other "future felicity," "it ought to be the endeavour of every man to derive his reflections from the objects about him," for, as Johnson says, guarding against the sort of fixation Piozzi assigned to him, "it is to no purpose that he alters his position, if his attention continues fixed to the same point" (3:28). The essay, which is appearing in early April, makes clear how especially conducive to such presence of mind is the spring, which "affords to a mind, so free from the disturbance of cares or passions as to be vacant to calm amusements, almost every thing that our present state makes us capable of enjoying" (3:27). The way to fill our vacuity is to empty our minds (make them "vacant to calm amusements").

Even more ironically, the exuberance of this celebration of the spring—of the "variegated verdure of the fields and woods, the succession of grateful odours, the voice of pleasure pouring out its notes on every side, with the gladness apparently conceived by every animal"—verges not only on dismantling the first part of the essay, tending to justify the man who all but lost himself in continual dreams of "this delightful season" (3:27, 26), but also threatens to undermine Johnson's recurrent stress on vacuity. We need only change our outlook and perceive fullness and unity, Johnson implies. But this idea will stand only for the moment. After this rhetorical flowering in praise of spring Johnson's next sentence anticipates a reversal, making clear that the focus here is not only on those who lose the present by dreaming of the spring or some other "future felicity" but also on those who lose the present by being insensible of it in other ways: namely, those "to whom these scenes are able to give no delight, and who hurry away from all the varieties of rural beauty, to lose their hours, and divert their thoughts by cards, or assemblies, a tavern dinner, or the prattle of the day" (3:27).

The Rambler in fact paints many memorable scenes of such distracted restlessness. The next essay compares the desperation of a leisured family with nothing to do to that of "a trader on the edge of bankruptcy" (3:31). As Johnson effectively puts it in Rambler 5, "when a man cannot bear his own company there is something wrong." What precisely is wrong in such a case, we read, is either that "he feels a tediousness in life from the equipoise of an empty mind," always requiring some "external" stimulation, or that "some unpleasing ideas" threaten to consume him, such as "the remembrance of a loss, the fear of a calamity, or some other thought of greater horror" (3:27–28). We may speculate (Johnson wants us to speculate) on what sort of "greater horror" might be conceived—a horror that, with the exclusion of memories and fears, must imply some cosmic or apocalyptic danger.

The antidote for such unhappiness is to avoid "an empty mind" and a reliance on external stimulation—precisely what the foregoing seemed to advocate. "The productions of nature," at least for the "man that has formed the habit of turning every new object to his entertainment," conveniently offer "an inexhaustible stock of materials upon which he can employ himself." But the question is at least potentially raised whether such an engagement in nature involves us in external dependency. At least we may note how this engagement with nature avoids those temptations that arise when one's "judgment is much exercised upon the works of art" (3:29), thus implicitly linking this essay to the previous one's remarks on the "envy or malevolence" of critics. To this benefit of so innocently occupying the mind, Johnson adds what appear to be some secondary incentives. The man who studies nature "has always a certain prospect of discovering new reasons for adoring the sovereign author of the universe, and probable hopes of making some discovery of the benefit to others, or of profit to himself" (3:29). The ambiguity of "always a certain prospect" (always some chance, or always an inevitable outcome?) hints that his secondary, adventitious matter will actually prove to be primary.

The essay's conclusion picks up this hint, pointing toward a concern decidedly more profound than identifying a "fresh amusement" for "those who languish in health, and repine in plenty." Calling upon "the younger part of my readers, to whom I dedicate this vernal speculation," Johnson asks them "to make use at once of the spring of the year, and the spring of life," and to remember that "a blighted spring makes a barren year, and that the vernal flowers, however beautiful and gay, are only intended by nature as preparatives to autumnal fruits" (3:29–30). The gravity of this religious exhortation adorned in seasonal flowers and fruits unobtrusively echoes the essay's earlier implications yet at the same time creates more puzzles.

For one thing, the critique of the man who looked forward to spring, which threatened to unravel itself all along, has somehow become an injunction to look forward to "autumn." If this essay, suggesting we immerse ourselves in a present that we know to be insufficient, is really to help us to live more happily here and now, we must somehow make sense of the orientation it espouses. We are urged to be "vacant to calm amusements" such as the spring, and we are urged to avoid "the equipoise of an empty mind" (3:27). This image of mental equipoise and inaction has appeared previously in the series as an uncomfortable state to be avoided. The first essay finds "the reasons for arrogance and submission" to be "so nearly equiponderant" that Johnson must launch into the series or be stalled in the effort to decide, and the figure of Criticism in *Rambler* 3 similarly finds herself increasingly "poised" before works in which "beauties and faults appeared so equally mingled" that only Time can judge them. Like Mr. Rambler, Criticism avoids this paralysis, stops trying to decide, and moves on. *Rambler* 5 thus offers some reassuring if commonplace advice—do not think of the future, and think of the future—but if we look closely at what it says we must be concerned if not confused, especially if we read this essay alone. And so we press on, hoping some harmony will emerge.

Rambler 6 from the outset seems designed to ensure and deepen our disturbance, forcing us to confront the gap between this essay and the previous one, for it immediately contradicts what we have just read. "That man should never suffer his happiness to depend upon external circumstances, is one of the chief precepts of the Stoical philosophy" (3:30). Johnson immediately qualifies but essentially agrees with this precept, admitting that "absolute independence is ridiculous and vain," but "a mean flexibility to every impulse . . . is below the dignity of that mind, which . . . boasts its derivation from a celestial original, and hopes for an union with infinite goodness and unvariable felicity" (3:31). The essay then turns, like the preceding one, to those "compelled to try all the arts of destroying time," briefly telling the story of a family who viewed an unexpected visitor "as provision to a starving city," enabling them "to hold out till the next day" when they must look for some other diversion (3:31–32). As *Rambler* 5 considers those who temporally absent themselves, looking to the spring, *Rambler* 6 considers those who refer their happiness to "change of place." Such spatial ramblers, like the imaginary time travellers, believe that "their pain is the consquence of some local inconveniences" and are "always hoping for more satisfactory delight from every new scene," only to be "always returning home with disappointment and complaints" (3:32).

The rest of this essay is then devoted to the illustrative case of Cowley, who, "however exalted by genius and enlarged by study," expressed the desire "to retire . . . to some of our American plantations," a "scheme of happiness" so absurd that "the imagination of a girl, upon the loss of her first lover, could have scarcely" concocted it. Cowley could have found as much solitude and solace as "the woods or fields of America" might offer, Johnson says, "within the limits of his native island" (3:34). If the preceding essay has suggested we might find happiness by absorbing ourselves in the "vegetables and animals" of spring (3:29), this essay (silently) contradicts or corrects that notion. Cowley has forgotten "that solitude and quiet owe their pleasures to those miseries" they oppose. It is the difference of "day and night, labour and rest, hurry and retirement," that we appreciate (3:34). More important, especially in view of the preceding essay and the stagnation of equipoise, we read that the motion of oscillating between these binary oppositions—deconstructing our lives we might say—serves to keep "the mind in action" (3:34–35). But Cowley, whose "passions were not sufficiently regulated," allowed his mind to focus only upon one alternative, privileging heavily secluded retirement. If like Cowley one forgets "that the fountains of content must spring up in the mind," and one should "seek happiness by changing anything, but his own disposition," then Johnson concludes he will "waste his life in fruitless efforts," perhaps recalling to the mind of the attentive reader the "autumnal fruits" at the end of the preceding essay. While *Rambler* 5 offers the useful advice of attending to the spring, it is advice that ultimately does not offer any final solution, as the extreme case of Cowley shows, foolishly trying to retire to a sort of geographical springtime.

After this effective attack on Cowley's wish for a bucolic retirement Johnson's reader may be surprised (his or her attention reawakened) to find the seventh essay begin by asserting that "those minds . . . most enlarged by knowledge, or elevated by genius," have "in all ages" loved "Retirement" (3:36). With no explicit reference to the prior ridicule of Cowley's retirement or his own urging that one should "derive his reflections from the objects about him" (3:28), Johnson puts forth the contrary or at least complementary idea that the intelligent man will "seek for that variety in his own ideas, which the objects of sense cannot afford him" (3:36). He then praises retirement, which not only is necessary to study, which is in turn necessary to knowledge, but is also "now especially" (in early April, approaching Easter) a sacred obligation, as "the institutions of the church" provide "an universal reason for stated intervals of solitude" (3:37). Johnson here articulates an axiom that suggests some way to pull together the foregoing, explaining the necessity of retirement but also reflecting as well on the danger of thinking too much on retirement: "We are in danger from whatever can get possession of our thoughts" (3:38). He is thereby able to reinforce the necessity of deriving our refections from the objects about us, as well as the danger of depending upon "external circumstances."

This danger is related to the recurrent image of equipoise, which might be seen as deconstruction carried to exhaustion, revealing why we should repeatedly retire.

> Thus it appears, upon a philosophical estimate, that, supposing the mind, at any certain time, in an equipoise between the pleasures of this life, and the hopes of futurity, present objects falling more frequently into the scale would in time preponderate, and that our regard for an invisible state would grow every moment weaker, till at least it would lose all its activity, and become absolutely without effect. (3:39)

Living in a binary opposition, pulled by "contrary attractions" (3:39), our lives are placed in an unstable orbit that without intervention is inevitably falling toward pleasures and "present objects." "The great art therefore of piety," Johnson says, "is the perpetual renovation of the motives to virtue," and retirement allows us to "weaken the temptations of the world"—"its [the world's] influence arising from its presence" (3:40). This "presence" is a function of our personal loss, highlighting the need to break the "perpetual" equipoise that is paradoxically always tending toward the "world" (an equipoise always going out of balance). By creating the artificial absence of retirement we can induce "a state, where this life, like the next, operates only upon the reason," a state that would constitute "the perfection of human nature" (3:40).

Such a posture, nullifying "present objects" and giving weight to "an invisible state" (3:39), may appear possible only for saints, demanding "fervent prayer, steady resolutions, and frequent retirement from folly and vanity." But the next essay, *Rambler* 8, offers

105

a view of the cosmos heartily encouraging to anyone striving to find an enduring presence through a temporary absence. The world, both time and space, is revealed in this essay to be in reality already virtually empty. Our thoughts are filled with "chasms . . . of wide and continued vacuity" and "interstitial spaces unfilled" (3:41). Thus the powerful forces drawing our time and attention away from piety in the prior essay are now shown to be in truth almost nonexistent.

In *Rambler* 8, especially within the Lockean and Newtonian context of a virtually vacuous space and time, it seems especially important to "govern our thoughts, restrain them from irregular motions, or confine them from boundless dissipation" (3:42). Otherwise, a "power so restless" as the human mind will "run to waste" (3:42). If we don't somehow grasp this empty here and evanescent now, we really do lose our minds and our selves and end up writing in our journals something akin to what Johnson wrote on Good Friday, 1764: "A kind of strange oblivion has overspread me, so that I know not what has become of the last year; and perceive that incidents and intelligence pass over me, without leaving any impression" (*Diaries* 1:77–78). All that separates us from being automatons, from being living computers, according to Marvin Minsky, pioneer of artificial intelligence, is our ability to "remember and record some of our thought processes" (58). Johnson likewise tells us that without such a memory trace we have no substantial consciousness, and *The Rambler* exhibits a variety of human automatons—Lady Busy, Lady Bustle, Mr. and Mrs. Courtly, Gulosulus, Gelidus, and others.

Thus Johnson's restatement of his purpose in *Rambler* 8, "to consider the moral discipline of the mind," takes on "the utmost importance." Without such discipline we become less than fully alive (we are in danger from whatever can control our thoughts). Johnson observes that "many acute and learned men" have considered how to amass knowledge, as if compiling data were the purpose of life, yet "the increase of virtue" has "been neglected for want of remembering that all action has its origin in the mind" (3:42). This oversight is amazing, but the neglected principle is so obvious that, as Johnson's psychology explains, it would easily be ignored. If it is of the "utmost importance" that we control our minds in order to control our actions, thus remaining alive in the profoundest sense, then retirement is essential. But *Rambler* 8 qualifies this prior endorsement (continuing the chain of contradictory/complementary wavering) by pointing out how the imagination "may corrupt our hearts in the most recluse solitude" even more perniciously than in "the commerce of the world." Johnson thereby promises to show "what thoughts are to be rejected or improved, as they regard the past, present, or future" (3:43).

"The recollection of the past," we then read, "is only useful by way of revision for the future" (3:44). This restrictive displacement of the value of the past onto the future is made even more stringent when Johnson advises us to avoid reviewing a "guilty pleasure" until a time in the future when "the impressions of past pleasures" have lessened. So the past is valued here only in terms of the future and is even partially deferred to the future for contemplation. But in turning away we encounter another displacement. As we think about what is to come, "we ought, at least, to let our desires fix upon nothing in another's power for the sake of our quiet, or in another's possession for the sake of our innocence" (3:46). What can we desire under this restriction other than what we already have? This difficulty of imagining a future composed of what is already in our power and possession is further complicated by the contrary observation in *Rambler* 5 that a man who dreams of the future is "lucky . . . when he turns his hopes upon things wholly out of his own power" (3:26). Especially in view of Johnson's warning that futurity is chiefly where (or when) the "snares" of imagination "are lodged," perhaps we should try to avoid thinking of the future altogether. "Our quiet" and "our innocence" might best be protected by silence and imbecility—by a mind "vacant to calm amusement," as *Rambler* 5 has put it. But how do we differentiate such vacancy from the emptiness of Johnson's automatons and slaves of passion?

With this question we are driven to the here and now, which we have already seen is inherently empty. If we recall *Rambler* 5 and the "inlets of happiness" in nature, we may assume that thoughts on present things should be improved. If we recall *Rambler*

7 and "the descent to life merely sensual," we may assume they should be rejected. Having promised guidance on thoughts "past, present, or future," Johnson now puts off that task precisely because present thoughts are determined "by the objects before us" and therefore "fall not under those indulgences, or excursions, which I am now considering" (3:45). He does however say something in deferring:

> But I cannot forbear, under this head, to caution pious
> and tender minds, that are disturbed by the irruptions of
> wicked imaginations, against too great dejection, and too
> anxious alarms; for thoughts are only criminal, when
> they are first chosen, and then voluntarily continued.
> (3:45)

This caution, standing in place of the promised advice, continues the negation of the present moment by recommending we reject any wicked thoughts and also remove dejection and alarm, thereby moving us toward the "state of tranquillity" mentioned in *Rambler* 6.

What has this demanding succession of qualifications, reversals, and dispersions (and its rehearsal here for that matter) accomplished? As in this grouping of essays, throughout the series Johnson repeatedly sets up oppositions and qualifications, within, between, and among essays, opposing one position to another. Such tendencies have of course been noticed by other readers. Donald Greene observes for example that "a 'but' (or reiterated 'but') is a common feature of the essays" ("'Logical Structure'" 335). James Boyd White recognizes that "one essay will often respond to a conclusion reached in another, placing it in a slightly different light" (152). John Radner notes that "quite often, as in *Ramblers* 6 and 7, and in *Ramblers* 79 and 80, Johnson begins essays by completing or complementing, but not actually revising, the argument of the essay he finished a few days earlier" (147n.7). My analysis of the opening sequence of essays has tried to expand on such perceptions, suggesting how many essays react to

No, this perceive perverts & distorts such perceptions!

preceding essays, thus positing a complex of evolving relationships more extensive and coherent than has previously been noted. Reading forward we are enticed to read backward. Such connections proliferate throughout the series—which deserves to be seen as a series, not a collection of isolated essays. I think we now may see how Johnson is attempting to engage his reader's attention in the recovery and examination of familiar truths. As Johnson says in *Rambler* 87, "Every man of genius has some arts of fixing the attention peculiar to himself, by which honestly exerted, he may benefit mankind" (4:98). For Johnson that apparently involves creating striking gaps between and within essays—aporia that cancel the readers' natural tendency toward an absence of thought by involving them in contrast and (dis)connection.

But, more importantly, how do these essays and their contesting commonplaces fit together? Does Johnson leave the reader in confusion? No, not if we exercise "the great prerogative of man" and connect and relate his assertions. Looking over this set of essays, *Ramblers* 5–8, we find this progression: we should (*a*) avoid an empty mind and (*b*) attend to the here and now, specifically to the spring (*Rambler* 5); (*c*) we should not however depend entirely on the here and now, (*d*) but in restraining our desire we must at the same time avoid a total withdrawal, or a desire like Cowley's (*Rambler* 6); (*e*) instead, we should retire periodically to perceive the insufficiency of the present (*Rambler* 7); and (*f*) perceiving this temporal and spatial vacuity, we should regularly look to eternity—specifically to the eternal significance of the here and now (*Rambler* 8). This progression, broken by an act of faith or will (to see the eternal in the temporal), establishes an instructive paradigm for the series. It allows us to make sense of apparently contradictory assertions by placing them within this emerging cycle of desire.

For example, in a number of essays, as in *Rambler* 29, Johnson advocates "the secure possession of the present moment" (3:158). And yet we also encounter passages that disparage the degree to which we are enslaved to the present moment (see 4:6 for instance) or assert that "the great task of him, who conducts his life by the precepts of religion, is to make the future predominate over the present" (3:38). These contradictory directives can be easily harmonized by the familiar implications of the cycle of desire underlying the progression of the early *Ramblers*. Johnson's enthusiasm for journals versus his infatuation with the topic of life's vacuity is similarly resolved. We must fill the emptiness of the present moment by grasping it firmly in all of its eternal significance. Thus, keeping a journal is in several ways an attack upon the vacuity of the here and now as well as a preparation for eternity. But it is also a seemingly futile gesture at any given moment as the present is always already slipping away.

If Johnson's great series comes down essentially to this familiar insight, it of course becomes then a collection of religious commonplaces. Yet Johnson himself apparently considered *The Rambler* to be an original endeavor. When he (re)announces his purpose in *Rambler* 8, "to consider the moral discipline of the mind, and to promote the increase of virtue rather than of learning," he continues, "This inquiry seems to have been neglected for want of remembering that all action has its origin in the mind, and that therefore to suffer the thoughts to be vitiated, is to poison the fountains of morality" (4:42). Johnson, not content to duplicate the achievements of his predecessors, chooses a uniquely ambitious goal for an essay series—nothing less than saving the reader's and his own soul by reminding us of fundamental truths, awakening us to their profundity and the need to apply them to our minds. What is novel and great about Johnson's series is the way he achieves this reawakening, arriving at familiar truths by rigorously dismantling settled assumptions. This dismantling leads us not by any direct or positively logical path but by a labyrinth of exclusions. We *must* believe, Johnson says; we must because otherwise the nothing that is continually appearing without our notice here and now means nothing. Even this fundamental and familiar axiom is continually slipping away from our inattentiveness—which is the reason Johnson's aim in the first essay must be declared seductively as "the entertainment of my countrymen." We are ramblers, and the "origin in the mind" of our actions, an origin that is emptying, is never stable, always in motion, wandering, requiring a series of essays in a quixotic quest.

"Distant Propositions by Regular Consequences"

To review and clarify Johnson's systematic view of time and space and to indicate further its pervasiveness and centrality, I want to discuss briefly some representative citations. Rather than following a sequence of essays I will select examples of the progression of desire from throughout the series.

Johnson insists repeatedly that we begin when we find ourselves in a present that is insufficient to our desires, a here and now that is really neither. "It has been remarked, perhaps, by every writer who has left behind him observations upon life, that no man is pleased with his present state," as *Rambler* 63 begins (3:334). In the penultimate essay Johnson is still reiterating this much-reiterated point. It begins: "Such is the emptiness of human enjoyment, that we are always impatient of the present. Attainment is followed by neglect, and possession by disgust" (5:310). It is "that insatiable demand of new gratifications," Johnson says in *Rambler* 80, "which seems particularly to characterize the nature of man" (4:56). This absence we must remember to notice; it is a nothing full of significance.

If we cannot somehow deal with this entropy of pleasure, the natural dissipation of our attention and contentment that we experience again and again in *The Rambler* as in our lives, then we face dire consequences, as in the case of Almamoulin in *Rambler* 120. "Change of place at first relieved his satiety, but all the novelties of situations were soon exhausted; he found his heart vacant, and his desires, for want of external objects, ravaging himself" (4:278). As *Rambler* 85 succinctly concludes, "to be idle is to be vicious" (4:86). Like Almamoulin and many others, Euphelia in *Rambler* 42 finds herself "languishing in a dead calm for want of some external impulse," as "the current of youth stagnates" (3:231), and Victoria in *Rambler* 133 similarly discovers her "every receptacle of ideas empty," as her mind assumes a "motionless indifference" (4:344). We must somehow make some difference. We must, returning to the schema above, (*a*) avoid an empty mind.

It is also possible to arrive at the stagnation of an empty mind by thinking too much. The writer who faces many possible solutions to any particular problem feels like a ship "impelled at the same time by opposite winds," as in *Rambler* 23 (3:130), and the scholar who finds "books of every kind around me" in *Rambler* 132 risks a "perpetual equipoise" (4:336). If we choose one thing we lose the other, and we find inevitably that our choice is different from itself, never fulfilling our aim. As we deliberate under such conditions, deconstructing our autonomy, our options, we must find what even "mechanicks have long discovered," as *Rambler* 153 says, "that contrariety of equal attractions is equivalent to rest" (5:49). Yet such is our nature.

Of course, we may combat this always-already-present vacuity if we (*b*) attend to the here and now, attempting "the secure possession of the present hour," as Johnson reminds us the ancient poets advised (*Rambler* 29; 3:158). *Rambler* 124 tells us "every moment produces something new to him, who has quickened his faculties by diligent observation" (4:299). As we rely upon external things to fill our attention, however, we run the risk of sinking into "the chains of sensuality," as *Rambler* 110 puts it (4:225). In fact, according to *Rambler* 70, "most minds are the slaves of external circumstances" (4:6). Thus we repeatedly must (*c*) withdraw from the present, retire and contemplate our situation. "The present is seldom able to fill desire or imagination with immediate enjoyment, and we are forced to supply its deficiencies by recollection or anticipation" (*Rambler* 203; 5:291). Such retirement is healthy: as *Rambler* 89 says, "all have agreed that our amusements should not terminate wholly in the present moment, but should contribute more or less to future advantage" (4:108). We must think ahead, as *Rambler* 117 says, for "all industry must be excited by hope" (4:259). Alternately, as *Rambler* 41 asserts, the past contains "the only joys which we can call our own" (3:224); and the dying man in *Rambler* 54 finds that only "the memory of acts of goodness" or "the duties of religion" brought him comfort (3:291).

At the same time, we must (*d*) avoid immersing ourselves in retirement and speculation past and future. Cupidus in *Rambler* 73 is so "accustomed to give the future full power" over his mind that he has been "corrupted with an inveterate disease of wishing"

(4:22). Conversely, young people like Rhodoclia in *Rambler* 62 have no memories to draw upon and must therefore be impatient without some immediate pleasure. Even for those who have done some living, the satisfactions of the past are necessarily a function of the substance of our lives; for someone like Gulosulus (and who is not a little like him?) "the only commonplaces of his memory are his meals" (5:309).

We must therefore (*e*) perceive the insufficiency of our lives at present. The most dramatic and conclusive sign of that inadequacy is, obviously, death. *Rambler* 178 even defines "life" as "that particle of our duration which is terminated by the grave" (5:174). *Rambler* 78 offers a direct version of a pervasive theme: "The remembrance of death ought to predominate in our minds, as an habitual and settled principle, always operating, though not always perceived" (4:47). With our capacities, no principle could always continually be perceived, and therefore we face, as Johnson says, "the perpetual renovation of the motives to virtue" (3:40)—which involves inevitably confronting "the end of our existence" (*Rambler* 80; 4:59). It is this ultimate vacuity, this final aporia, that particularly leads to the unfounded meaning of the absent, empty present—and faith. Johnson's faith arises out of the most profound difference (between our desires and our lives) and deferral (of contentment).

Thus Johnson leads us to return our attention to the present, but not entirely to the present, taking a double vision, as we (*f*) act now thinking of eternity. As Johnson says in *Rambler* 78, "Our attention should seldom wander so far from our condition as not to be recalled and fixed by the sight of an event, which must soon, we know not how soon, happen likewise to ourselves, and of which, though we cannot appoint the time, we may secure the consequence" (4:47–48). Of course, our attention does inevitably wander. Even trying to tell the most uncomplicated story, "simple narration" as Johnson says in *Rambler* 122, involves us "in wilds and mazes, in digression and confusion" (4:287). But the effort to "secure the consequence" creates out of this errant state, as the Sage tells Obidah in *Rambler* 120, "the only happiness ordained for our present state," which must be based upon "the confidence of divine favor, and the hope of future rewards" (4:280). As *Rambler*

69 puts it, "Piety is the only proper and adequate relief of decaying man" (3:367). Belief, Johnson believes, is the only thing that works, that produces "a settled conviction of the tendency of everything to our good" (*Rambler* 32; 3:179). *Rambler* 180 is just one of many exhortations, this one directed particularly to "the candidates of learning," who should cease "wandering after the meteors of philosophy" and fix "their eyes upon the permanent lustre of moral religious truth" (5:186)—upon a mazing and amazing grace.

4

"The Order in Which They Stand": (Re)Writing Johnson (Re)Writing

> I have also studied metaphysicks. I know the arguments for fate and free-will, for the materiality and immateriality of the soul, and even the subtle arguments for and against the existence of matter. . . . But let us leave these disputes to the idle. . . . I hold always one great object. I never feel a moment of despondency.
>
> —Paoli qtd. in Boswell

"So Far Arbitrary and Immethodical"

Deconstruction both elevates and depreciates criticism. In the version of deconstruction celebrated by Geoffrey Hartman, the critic invents the text, creatively revealing possibilities that are always in excess of any particular formulation, releasing and dispersing its meaning. But the dark side of deconstruction, as Paul de Man has painstakingly shown, also requires that the critic give up any claim to priority because his or her reading is unavoidably a misreading awaiting exposure, a mastery made possible only by a prejudicial subjugation of some subjects at the expense of others. Johnson's awareness of these alternative aspects of criticism, of its blindness and insight, can be seen in his comment on Warburton's discovery of "order and connection" in Pope's *Essay on Man*. "Almost every poem consisting of precepts, is so far arbitrary and immethodical, that many of the paragraphs may change places with no apparent inconvenience. . . . But for the order in which they stand, whatever it be, a little ingenuity may easily give a reason" (*Lives* 3:99). As Johnson indicates here, the critic's ingenuity is validated by the freeplay of writing, in which even preceptive poems are formed by an "arbitrary and immethodical" *dispositio* (the openness of Hartman's deconstruction). But to exercise his creativity, to account for the work's order, the critic must ignore precisely this same infinitude of form (the discipline of de Man's version). The critic is alternatively empowered by only "a little ingenuity" and restricted to only "a little ingenuity."

Johnson's modern critics can hardly be accused of wanting the cleverness to posit "order and connection" in his works. Yet according to an impressive array of Johnsonians—Fussell, Knoblauch, O'Flaherty, Curley, Alkon, Pierce, Greene, Damrosch—the characteristic structuring of Johnson's writing is "extemporaneous," "ad hoc," "arbitrary," exploratory, "inductive," "rambling, disorderly," struggling, "illogical," "loose," "associative," and even "almost Shandean."[1] It would be remarkable if this surprising critical consensus regarding the movement of Johnson's discourse has not been influenced, at least in part, by the memorable anecdotes of Johnson's last-minute, impatient, unplanned approach to composing (not to mention his dishevelled dress and edacious eating). The classic instance of Johnson's practice is Hester Piozzi's revelation that the famous essay on procrastination, *Rambler* 134, was "hastily composed in Sir Joshua Reynolds' parlour, while the boy waited to carry it to press" (178). Also familiar is Bennet Langton's memory, recorded by Boswell, of how Johnson while visiting Oxford sat down thirty minutes before the mail left for London and "finished an *Idler*, which it was necessary should be in London the next day." When Langton asked to read it, Johnson replied that "you shall not do more than I have done myself," and "folded it up, and sent it off" (1:331).

Johnson's eccentric personality and extraordinary genius certainly make the idea that he dashed off his works at the last second seem both plausible and appealing. Perceiving the inherently "arbitrary and immethodical" nature of writing would appear to justify such a free-flowing practice. By positing a Johnson whose writing reflects the anxious, unpremeditated circumstances of its production, Johnson's critics in effect have already seen his discourse in a partially deconstructive light in which Johnson's texts turn against themselves and language masters his purpose. This, I suggest, is too much insight, and my aim in this chapter will involve obscuring our vision of Johnson's compositional freedom by focusing on his constraints and control in the act of writing, in structuring essays, and in sequencing them. This control stems from Johnson's own deconstructive insight and the chosen blindness of his faith.

We might first acknowledge that there is something troubling about the classic example of Johnson's haste, Hester Piozzi's story of *Rambler* 134. Why was Johnson composing his essay on procrastination "in Sir Joshua Reynolds' parlour, while the boy waited to carry it to press," when Johnson did not yet know Reynolds, whom he would not meet until after the *Rambler* had ended?[2] Reynolds also appears to have been in France and Italy throughout its publication. Johnson must have really waited until the last second if he had to break into the parlor of someone absent and unknown. If this particular story is incorrect in some way, what about all the other anecdotes of Johnson's last-minute writing, including those reportedly told by the author himself? Could they all be mistaken, exaggerated, or distorted in some way? If these stories are too numerous to be entirely fictional—and one must admit after all that Piozzi may have just misplaced the parlor—then the widespread retailing of Piozzi's story without challenge may still alert us to a more significant point: her anecdote, besides possibly being too good to be true, has been so often repeated because it supports the construction of a mythic Johnson.[3] Rather than attempt to question all these second- and third-hand anecdotes, which is quite probably impossible at this time, perhaps we should reconsider their significance. What do we really know about how Johnson worked? What do these stories, including Piozzi's, really tell us about the measure of planning and revision and control Johnson exercised in his writing? How else might we account for such narratives of last-minute writing?

Bishop Percy, Johnson's good friend, offers us another view in a remarkably neglected "revelation," as he puts it, of how Johnson wrote. Percy claims that Johnson, hating to use pen and paper because of his poor eyesight, composed and polished his pieces orally, holding them in memory until he was forced to commit them to paper (215–16). In his *Life of Pope* Johnson mentions such a remarkable manner of writing as if it were simply a common alternative to writing with pen and paper (*Lives* 2:218). Gibbon in fact reveals that "it has always been my practise to cast a long paragraph in a single mould, to try it by my ear, to deposit it in my memory, but to suspend the action of the pen, till I had given the last polish to my work" (159). This method may seem to us to require astonishing feats of memory, but Pope, Gibbon, Johnson, and many others in the eighteenth century were still very much immersed in classical rhetoric, in which memory and internal composition played a crucial role. The manuscript of *The Vanity of Human Wishes* indicates, as the Yale editors note, that Johnson composed all of that poem "before any of it was set down, and it was then written rapidly" (*Poems* 6:90–91). Boswell in fact reports Johnson's remark that in writing verses, "I have generally had them in mind, perhaps fifty at a time, walking up and down in a room; and then I have written them down, and often, from laziness, have written only half lines" (2:15). When Boswell regretted that Johnson "had not given us more of Juvenal's Satires," Johnson replied, according to Boswell, "he probably should . . ., for he had them all in his head" (1:193).

Not only is it possible that Johnson often developed and refined his essays without pen and paper but there is also substantial evidence that he prepared in advance. As James Clifford has observed, Payne and Cave advertised some forthcoming issues in various London newspapers by printing their Latin (and in one instance Greek) mottoes. Clifford concludes:

> If it was his practice to dash off the essays in haste and send them to the printers without even rereading what he had produced, at least the motto must have been decided upon earlier, in time to be inserted in the next

morning's newspaper advertisement. If the motto had been chosen well in advance, then the general theme must also have been known to the printers. The early reports of haste may have been exaggerated. (77)

Clifford, however, does not really embrace the idea that the reports of haste were exaggerated, for a few pages later he reminds us "that the first versions, which were the ones perused by readers in 1750, were hasty compositions, usually tossed off without careful revision" (83). He adds on the next page, reinforcing Boswell's portrait of Johnson's eccentric genius, that "actually it is remarkable that the style throughout was as good as it was, when pieces were dashed off at such speed" (84).

More important than the advance selection of mottoes is the evidence that Johnson regularly relied on written notes and drafts. Boswell asserts his possession of "a small duodecimo volume" in which Johnson had written, "in the form of Mr. Locke's Common-Place Book, a variety of hints for essays on different subjects" (1:204). Although Boswell is clearly interested in promoting Johnson's mythic ability to write extemporaneously, the very existence of this volume calls such last-minute writing heroics into question. Since Boswell's rival, Sir John Hawkins, had already printed two specimens from Johnson's drafting, Boswell can hardly ignore these materials and still claim superior access to Johnson's documentary remains. Therefore Boswell presents Johnson's substantial outlines for *Rambler* 196 and *Adventurer* 45. The sketch of *Rambler* 196, employing fragments, phrases, and abbreviations, runs to over 350 words. Boswell's immediate comment on these materials seems especially odd without some grasp of his rhetorical problem.

> This scanty preparation of materials will not, however, much diminish our wonder at the extraordinary fertility of his mind; for the proportion which they bear to the number of essays which he wrote, is very small; and it is remarkable, that those for which he made no preparation, are as rich and as highly finished as those for which the hints were lying by him. (1:207–8)

These materials hardly appear, as Boswell calls them, "scanty." On the contrary, Johnson seems to have planned these two essays with some care, and the differences between drafts and published versions underscore a thoughtful process of development. On the first blank page of the particular volume in Boswell's possession Johnson has written, according to Boswell, "To the 128th page, collections for the RAMBLER" (1:204). These materials, Boswell notes, are written "in an exceedingly small hand" (1:208n.1), so it seems clear that we are talking about a considerable amount of material, especially when we consider also that a word or a phrase might stand as a reminder for sentences or paragraphs. Boswell also reports that a note "in another place" in the volume says that thirty *Ramblers*, in the sequence up to *Rambler* 190, were "taken from provided materials" in this volume (1:204).

If thirty essays were developed out of this volume then Johnson did not always write without preparation. How many other commonplace books did Johnson own? It seems quite implausible that he owned only one, and since other essays obviously might have been planned in other volumes, or on separate sheets, or on napkins for that matter, it is clear that Boswell actually cannot say with any authority that "the proportion" of preparatory materials to finished essays "is very small." When Boswell visited Johnson's library (in "two garrets over his Chambers"), he found the floor "strewed with manuscript leaves, in Johnson's own hand-writing," and he supposed, "with a degree of veneration," "they perhaps might contain portions of the *Rambler*, or of *Rasselas*" (1:435–36). If drafts of *Rambler* papers were still lying on the floor in 1763, Johnson's study really was, as Boswell says, "in great confusion." At any rate we know that "a great mass" of Johnson's papers were burned right before his death, and it is certainly reasonable to assume that various notes and drafts would be among those plentiful papers.

Boswell not only attempts to deflect the implications of this evidence he can hardly avoid presenting, he also uses (once again) this occasion to undermine Hawkins. First he asserts that Hawkins, "who is unlucky upon all occasions," has mistakenly compared Johnson's method of "accumulating intelligence" to Addison's

(1:208n.1). Boswell's comment that "there is no resemblance at all between them" is clearly incorrect. As Hawkins says, Addison's method "is humorously described" in *Spectator* 46, in which he pretends he has dropped "his paper of *notanda*, consisting of a diverting medley of broken sentences and loose hints, which he tells us he has collected, and meant to make use of" (266; cited by Boswell as "p. 268"). Boswell tells us that "Addison's note was a fiction, in which unconnected fragments of his lucubrations were purposely jumbled together, in as odd a manner as he could, in order to produce a laughable effect" (1:205). Hawkins obviously realizes that Addison offers a comical parody of his actual method, which seems to be essentially the same as Johnson's if the Johnsonian samples we have are representative. Boswell also charges that Hawkins in presenting his samples of Johnson's preparations has erroneously deciphered Johnson's handwriting. On this point we cannot judge, other than to observe Boswell's aggressive self-promotion: *he* can read Johnson's difficult hand.

My point here is that Boswell's rhetoric may distract us from the questionableness of his conclusions. Although Boswell claims "it is remarkable, that those for which he had made no preparation, are as rich and as highly finished as those for which the hints were lying by him" (1:207–8), no one in actuality can possibly say with confidence which essays, if any, were produced with "no preparation." It may be objected that the question of how Johnson wrote and whether he planned ahead is immaterial—that Johnson's text is the same no matter what we think of its production. But such an objection is unrealistic. The importance of the reader's assumptions is elegantly demonstrated by Stanley Fish's little experiment in which his students richly interpreted a poem that was in actuality a list of names left on the blackboard from the previous class (322–37). Their understanding that the text was a designed work which would repay their analysis was crucial to the production of that analysis.

In the case of Johnson's essay on procrastination, it is easy to see how Paul Fussell's perception of Johnson characteristically "caught short at deadline time," reduced to "working things out *ad*

121

hoc from page to page" in "frantic composition" (161, 160), shapes his reading of any particular essay. *Rambler* 134 is one of many essays, Fussell says, that Johnson must end "in quite a different mode from the one in which he began it" (160), forced to "virtually retract in the final paragraphs what he has set forth with every appearance of confidence early on" (161). Uncertain of what he means to say, Johnson finds his topic by writing, much like the student in freshman English who is told by the currently prevailing pedagogy to "write before writing."[4] In this essay and many others, Fussell tells us, Johnson's "real doubts and uncertainties are constantly at war with the mere appearance of order and faith" (160–61).

Fussell is one of Johnson's most engaging and stimulating modern readers. But if we start from the contrary assumption, imagining that Johnson thought through this essay as a rhetorical instrument, we immediately may begin to question Fussell's reading by noticing that he assumes the "I" in *Rambler* 134 is Johnson, and that "Johnson" was "now necessitated to write" in a real historical moment that precluded foresight and control. Johnson's repeated concern for the disabling effects of linking the author to his work is validated by Fussell's assumption, which overlooks the uncertain status of Mr. Rambler, and "Johnson" for that matter. The audience's writer, to reverse Walter Ong's axiom, is always a fiction.

Thus, "Mr. Rambler" and "Johnson" cannot be equated in any simple and direct fashion, and the essay for all we know may have been revised several times the day it was composed or worked on for months—or, given Johnson's powers, written in a thoughtful and concentrated burst, even at the last second. It is in fact easy enough to suggest how this essay develops logically and even how it reflects ideas raised in the preceding essays and throughout the series.

In the opening scene Mr. Rambler reports "deliberating" on various subjects and finding that his "ideas wandered from the first intention," leaving him with nothing accomplished, until he is "awakened from this dream of study by a summons from the press" (4:345). Such restless and ineffectual rambling, followed by an awakening to responsibility, is arguably the most recurrent and most important movement of the series. It defines, within *The Rambler* at least, the human condition. In the preceding issue, number 133, Victoria reveals how after smallpox has ruined her beauty she finds "every receptacle of ideas empty," despite a devoted search for "entertainment" (4:342). Like Mr. Rambler she is fortunately awakened from what she calls a "motionless indifference" by Euphemia, who exhorts her to "rise at once from your dream of melancholy to wisdom and piety" (4:344–45). Even the prior essay, *Rambler* 132, reflects this paradigm, as the scholar Eumathes finds that "unlimited inquiry" of the sort Mr. Rambler will confess two essays later results in "a perpetual equipoise," a suspension in which "the mind fluctuates between different purposes without determination" (4:336).

Fortunately, Mr. Rambler has "only trifled till diligence was necessary" which, he congratulates himself, is better than "multitudes, who have trifled till diligence is vain" (4:346). In other words, as is so often the case in *The Rambler*, writing is an analogy for living, and Johnson's readers must consider as this essay develops whether in their own lives diligence is now necessary or vain. Although "multitudes" are said to be in that state in which "no degree of activity or resolution" can recover opportunites or evade "hopeless calamity and barren sorrow," surely the reader is not so forlorn. The essay offers considerable hope and encouragment, telling us we can, even at this late date, do something constructive.

Indeed, Johnson asserts, "To act is far easier than to suffer" (4:347). So why do we fail to act, even though we also face an inevitable deadline? For the analogous reasons that we fail to write, Johnson reveals. On the one hand we may be paralyzed by fear or distracted by corruption, or we may simply "freeze in idleness" (4: 348). While doing nothing might appear to insulate us from fears and corruption, "idleness never can secure tranquillity" because even "the sluggard" cannot entirely escape "the call of reason and of conscience." On the other hand, like the writer, one may find "many objects of persuit arise at the same time," tempting us to wander ineffectually and ultimately to "pause in the choice of his road, till some accident interrupts his journey" (4:348). Just as anyone who waits until he knows everything fully and certainly will "never conclude himself qualified to write" (4:349), by the same token we cannot wait to determine our choice of life until we know everything about life. We must go ahead and live. And the "certainty that life cannot be long, and the probability that it will be much shorter than nature allows, ought to awaken every man to the active prosecution of whatever he is desirous to perform" (4:349). Although "death may intercept the swiftest career" nonetheless, the one "who is cut off in the execution of an honest undertaking, has at least the honor of falling in his ranks" (4:349).

According to Fussell, "Johnson ends *Rambler* 134 in quite a different mode from the one in which he began it" (160). This charge in itself seems hardly damaging: reversals and transitions are part of effective rhetorical strategies. But for Fussell this difference is evidence of Johnson's unpreparedness, confusion, and haste. "Instead of certainty or any sort of dogmatism," Fussell writes, "what we find in *Rambler* 134 is pathos, doubt, and the essential incertitude inseparable, we should notice, from the process of extemporaneous composition" (160). On the contrary, Johnson refers in his conclusion to "the certainty that life cannot be long" (the certainty of uncertainty), which "ought to" awaken us all. I fail to see how Johnson's "ought to" here, as Fussell suggests, stands as evidence of his "real doubts and uncertainties," "constantly at war with the mere appearance of order and faith" (160). Indeed, our doubts and uncertainties ought to compel us toward faith. Johnson says "ought to" because he realizes not everyone will act, even in the face of the most serious deadline: but we all should. The essay so beautifully incorporates the particular experience of Mr. Rambler, awakened from his rambling inactivity into the paradigm of all writers who delay (which in turn illustrates the all-inclusive class of anyone who procrastinates), that it is difficult to imagine how Fussell could fail to see the essay's confident and coherent moral exhortation— difficult until we recognize his insistence that Johnson's stance is "inseparable" from his composing process, which Fussell is convinced he fully comprehends.

The stories of how Johnson committed his works to paper— hurriedly, at the last minute—may tell us something about the construction of the public "Samuel Johnson" as an extraordinary genius and eccentric personality, but these narratives do not necessarily reveal his manner of composing. Nor, more significantly, do they supply any privileged access to his completed texts. Given Johnson's remarkable conversational abilities, his widely noted ability to "speak *Ramblers*" as Piozzi put it (347n.3), even his extemporaneous writing may be masterfully planned and controlled.[5] According to Boswell, Johnson told Reynolds

> that he had early laid it down as a fixed rule to do his best on every occasion, and in every company; to impart whatever he knew in the most forcible language he could put it in; and that by constant practice, and never suffering any careless expressions to escape him, or attempting to deliver his thoughts without arranging them in the clearest manner, it became habitual to him. (1:204).

If Johnson took such care with his conversation from "early on," it seems especially unlikely he would have willingly allowed sloppy, hasty thinking to get into print.

If we set aside the idea that Johnson's essays are a record of his eccentric composing process, their form may then be seen as the effect of some "arbitrary and immethodical" essence of language itself. As *Rambler* 122 says, "It is never easy, nor often possible, to comprise the series of any process, with all its circumstances, incidents, and variations, in a speculative scheme" (4:287). The previous chapter has dealt with this possibility to some degree, arguing that some recurrent deconstructive themes partially illuminate and distinguish Johnson's *Rambler*. The present chapter considers more specifically the movement of Johnson's thought, and the critical consensus in this regard immediately suggests a similar approach—namely, that Johnson's critics have already placed his *dispositio* in a deconstructive light. Again deconstruction may alert us to some neglected aspects of Johnson's *dispositio*, but that movement is really Johnson's positioning of the reader. For *The Rambler*

125

in my view is a rhetorical instrument and not (merely) the record of Johnson's composing, or the effect of a loss of faith in language (or any other realm), or the unavoidable consequence of language's impotence. We might note that the assertion in *Rambler* 122 of how difficult it is to analyze a process functions as part of a carefully plotted essay. Johnson is talking about the unsuspected difficulty of performing tasks that appear to be easy, a misjudgment often arising when "we form our opinion from the performances of others"—from the spectacular success of a predecessor, for instance (4:286). Johnson is especially interested here in the writing of history, for nothing appears "so artless or easy as simple narration" (4:287). Yet even this endeavor, Johnson says, much attuned to the slippage of signifiers, involves us in "wilds and mazes, in digression and confusion." When historical writing succeeds, it is remarkable; and Knolles "has displayed all the excellencies that narration can admit" (4:290). Unfortunately, Johnson concludes, Knolles has chosen a topic, the history of the Turks, "of which none desire to be informed" (4:291), virtually wasting his talent and effort. The larger significance of this observation is implied earlier when Johnson points to the "many things" in life that falsely appear easy and "promise certainty of success to our next essay" (4:207), linking life and writing.

In fact, as Johnson describes the author's task and the reader's mind, the widespread perception that his writing rambles may be seen as a sign of at least the partial success of his rhetoric. If the author's task regarding moral discipline involves recommending known truths, and the reader is naturally restless, in search of novelty, resistant to the very familiar ideas Johnson is striving to bring to his attention, then immediate perceptions of inevitability, of expectedness, would obviously be unproductive. The author of *The Rambler* finds himself in a situation not entirely unlike Knolles's, taking up a topic in which few are really interested, familiar moral truths. As the critical response makes clear, Johnson's readers have certainly been startled by the movement of his essays, so much so they have doubted his foresight and control. For Leopold Damrosch our surprise and confusion are the purpose of Johnson's essays, which strive "to disturb the complacency" of readers, sparking

126

inquiry and deepening understanding by a series of disjunctions and associations (82, 85).

In what follows I build on Damrosch's insight and suggest how the reader's experience of particular essays pushes him or her to confront the rationality of faith.[6] This purpose, which is equivalent to the moral discipline of the mind, is best served by a series of essays, for faith (or discipline) is not a state we enter and enjoy securely, at least for Johnson. The natural entropy of contentment applies to belief, and so Johnson is faced with the task of repeatedly and unexpectedly and differently breaking down the barriers to a clear understanding of who we are and what life is for. Again I argue that deconstruction's wake provides a useful and limiting perspective that is again complemented by an eighteenth-century context, as Johnson both inhabits and surpasses eighteenth-century ideas of logic and rhetoric.

If the *dispositio* of individual essays deserves closer analysis, what about the positioning of the reader in the sequencing of essays? We have already seen unstated connections, or strategically open spaces, between *Ramblers* 1–4 and 5–8, and my consideration of Johnson's rhetoric will include further discussion of this neglected aspect of the series, the relationship of essays both contiguous and remote.

"To Regulate One Part of Our Composition by Some Regard to the Other"

Let us imagine a reader situated in *Rambler* 24, an essay that reminds us of an extraordinarily familiar precept, "Be acquainted with thyself." Although no aphorism is "more famous among the masters of antient wisdom"; although it has been "admitted by general consent, and inculcated by frequent repetition"; still, according to the essay's motto from Persius, it is universally ignored: "Nemo in sese tentat descendere" ("No one attempts to descend into himself"). The motto is characteristically resonant. Persius is advising Alcibiades to ignore the mob and simply be himself, which is precisely Johnson's point in the preceding essay. There, in *Rambler* 23, Mr. Rambler finds himself amid a "tumult of criticism, as a ship in a poetical tempest, impelled at the same time by opposite winds" (3:130). The writer, especially the essayist, faces "a boundless variety" of approaches that threaten to trap him "in perpetual suspense between contrary impulses." Unable to decide questions within the unbounded realm of language, in which a different approach might always be taken, something else might always be said, the writer may "consult for ever without determination" (3:126). Mr. Rambler will avoid this deconstructive meltdown that recurrently arises in the series by striving "to gain the favor of the publick" in a paradoxical and characteristic way—by claiming to ignore them, as Persius suggests, and "following the direction of my own reason" and "indulging the sallies of my own imagination" (3:130).

To make this self-isolating and self-disclosing move, Mr. Rambler must in a sense repeat the error of his dissatisfied reader who "lets his imagination rove at large, and wonders that another, equally unconfined in the boundless ocean of possibility, takes a different course" (3:128). Mr. Rambler must release within himself the force that he decries in others, as the antidote to indulged imagination seems to be in part indulging the imagination; he must also seek success by repudiating it. The "publick, which is never corrupted, nor often deceived, is to pass the last sentence upon literary claims" (3:128), but the public must be ignored if he is to choose to write anything at all. Neither of these contrary moves can be completed. His imagination must be checked by his reason; the act of writing in itself reinstates the audience he is trying to ignore. A controlled rambling is the only solution.

For the author who decides to follow his own mind, the precept under scrutiny in Rambler 24, know thyself, is obviously crucial. In fact, all the foregoing advice in The Rambler can be said to hinge on this directive. Rambler 9, for instance, first exposes the "very strong and active prejudice" most men have "in favour of their own vocation." Although this zeal produces a "thousand ridiculous and mischievous acts of supplantation and detraction," as the first part of this essay points out, it also "excites ingenuity, and sometimes raises an honest and useful emulation of diligence" (3:48–49). Rather than extinguish "this passion for the honour of a profes-

128

sion," or indulge it, we should "regulate" it. We can oscillate between these alternatives only if we know ourselves, recognizing
our own bias.

We are similarly exhorted to regulate our passions in *Rambler*
11, which deals with anger; in *Rambler* 12, which deals with
"thoughtless vanity"; and in *Rambler* 13, which deals with keeping
secrets. Although controlling these passions consists of what Johnson calls a "negative" virtue, requiring inaction, these deceptively
simple situations "such as generally occur in common life" are
revealed to be surprisingly difficult. In the case of keeping secrets,
the analysis of how to behave inevitably will lead "the threads of
reasoning, on which truth is suspended," to be stretched to "such
subtility, that common eyes cannot perceive, and common sensibil-
ity cannot feel them" (3:73). As Johnson presents it, "The whole
doctrine as well as practice of secrecy, is so perplexing and dangerous, that, next to him who is compelled to trust, I think him unhappy who is chosen to be trusted" (3:73). To avoid being incapaci-
tated by his own rigorous analysis, Johnson turns away from the
impossibility of determining binding rules for keeping secrets and
supplies us with three principles "from which I think it not safe to
deviate, without long and exact deliberation" (a qualification that
threatens to launch more analysis): do not solicit secrets; resist
accepting such confidences; and consider such trusts, when unavoidably offered, "important as society and sacred as truth" (3:73).

Perhaps the most forceful motive to the silence, suspension,
introspection, and isolation Johnson recommends is, as *Rambler* 17
says, the "known shortness of life," which as we recognize it is
sure "to moderate our passions" and "contract our designs." We
must remember, Johnson says, "how much more our minds can
conceive, than our bodies can perform," and therefore, "while we
continue in this complicated state" of life, we must strive to regulate
one part of our composition by some regard to the other" (3:97).
Regulating our verbal "composition" involves a similar complementarity. *Rambler* 22 allegorically shows us how Wit and Learning,
ineffective singly, have "a numerous progeny of Arts and Sciences"
when married, a state that certainly involves having "some regard
to the other." Conversely, in *Rambler* 19 Polyphilus, a brilliant dab-

bler in everything as his name suggests, illustrates again the dangers of an unfettered analysis, of endlessly pitting one alternative against another without choosing. Polyphilus's talents are "dissipated in boundless variety" as he dismantles every career choice, and his experience is representative. Every man, Johnson asserts, who "balances the arguments on every side," will be forced at last "to rest in neutrality as the decision devolves into the hands of chance" (3:109).

Even the basis for "the regulation of life" (3:130), "Be acquainted with thyself," is subjected to this logic of unbounded analysis interrupted. This dictate, Johnson says in Rambler 24, which "in the whole extent of its meaning, may be said to comprise all the speculation requisite to a moral agent" (3:130), is actually a part that contains the whole—requiring nothing less than "the knowledge of our original, our end, our duties, and our relation to other beings." Since this knowledge is "necessary to the regulation of life," Johnson appears to have created at the outset an impossible scenario in which we must know everything about ourselves in order to begin to regulate any part of our lives, a hermeneutic circle in which we are the text and the subject.

Such an interpretive endeavor is obliquely mocked by Johnson's inability even to say who originated this precept (much less what our own origin might be), and the next sentence directly qualifies this impossibly totalizing principle, for "the first author, whoever he was," surely did not intend "this unlimited and complicated sense" (3:130–31). Some inquiries "are too extensive for the powers of man, and some require light from above, which was not yet indulged to the heathen world" (3:131). Part of the problem with limiting the precept, Johnson points out, is that we do not know its context. Did it originate as "a general instruction to mankind, or as a particular caution to some private inquirer"? There are, he continues, "many possible circumstances, in which this monition might very properly be inforced," which apparently tells us indirectly that this fundamental directive is not applicable in some other circumstances. The next paragraph, the sixth, seems to be discussing precisely those circumstances not affected, circumstances "too extensive for the powers of man" as Johnson has said earlier: "When a man employs himself upon remote and unncessary subjects, and wastes his life upon questions, which cannot be resolved and of which the solution would conduce very little to the advancement of happiness" (3:131). But as Johnson delineates this category further another picture begins to emerge, for those inquiries "when he lavishes his hours in calculating the weight of the terraqueous globe, or in adjusting successive systems of worlds beyond the reach of the telescope" (3:131), certainly do warrant recalling one to the directive "Be acquainted with thyself." Startlingly, one category, in which (self-) knowledge is unobtainable, has become the other, in which self-knowledge should be pursued. Even in the wilds and mazes of language we keep getting lost, which reveals where we are. This self-knowledge, telling us what we do not know and are not fit to know, is more a negation than a positive acquisition, but it is profoundly valuable nonetheless.

After observing that Socrates wisely turned man's attention from "the stars and tides" to "the various modes of virtue," and that "men of learning" still "study anything rather than themselves" (3:132), Johnson presents the character of Gelidus, a "great philosopher" who "has so far abstracted himself from the species, as to partake neither of the joys and griefs of others" (3:133). He "neglects the endearments of his wife, and the caresses of his children, to count the drops of rain, note the changes of the wind, and calculate the eclipses of the moons of Jupiter" (3:133–34). Interestingly, the directive to "know thyself" becomes, in the case of Gelidus, the complementary injunction to pay attention to others. But this entire discussion, Johnson says, is itself deferring a "religious and important meaning of this epitome of wisdom" that will occupy "some future paper" (3:134). The secular meaning is simply that the "absurdity of pride could proceed only from ignorance" of oneself (3:134), as is shown in the final part of this essay by the character of Euphues, an intelligent man who desires only "to distinguish himself by particularities in his dress," and in the essay's concluding reference to "the ladies," who forget their own age, pretending they are young (3:134, 135).

Such explicit connections between essays ("some future paper") involving Ramblers that are sometimes days apart, and sometimes even months, do actually occur fairly often in the series. Mr. Rambler casually refers in *Rambler* 175 to a point made "in a former paper" that turns out to be *Rambler* 79, published almost a year earlier; *Ramblers* 194 and 195 complete a story begun in number 132. In this case, the essay promised in *Rambler* 24 appears only two weeks later, in *Rambler* 28. The two linked essays are separated by the deployment of familiar themes and techniques that nonetheless produce some surprising effects in juxtaposition.

In *Rambler* 25 Johnson considers where we should position ourselves in relation to rashness and cowardice. "True fortitude," which should be our goal, is "equally distant" from these opposites, but staying in between does not involve avoiding both with equal effort. "Presumption will be easily corrected," Johnson tells us, but "timidity is a disease of the mind more obstinate and fatal" and especially pervasive in "men devoted to literature," who are prone to "a kind of intellectual cowardice." It is only by wavering in this middle state that we can see clearly "the difficulty of excellence," dampening our boldness, and "the force of industry," diminishing fear (3:140). To balance these opposites, Johnson says we should somehow favor presumption without falling into it—again, a difficult stance requiring constant (re-)attention.

Ramblers 26 and 27 reveal the character of Eubulus, who is hopelessly out of touch with himself and offends his protective uncle, making himself dependent on the favor of others. His situation is the analogue of the story of the author trying to please his readers in *Rambler* 23, as Eubulus finds "I was to comply with a thousand caprices, to concur in a thousand follies, and to countenance a thousand errors" (3:145). Unable to turn away, to withdraw, to choose decisively, he comes to realize "no word, or look, or action was my own" (3:146), as his individuality is dismantled. Once again the solution involves turning away from this deconstructive implosion. When his uncle dies, he determines to "retire to an humbler state," and as he writes he is "endeavouring to recover the dignity of virtue," which is based on self-direction.

Rambler 28, the promised religious essay, is powerful, pulling together Johnson's purpose. Again "retirement and abstraction" are presented as crucial moves. Johnson tells us that by disengaging from "sublunary hopes and fears" one may assign "proper portions of his life to the examination of the rest." In such analysis we should not mistake single acts for habits, or habits for single acts, and (perhaps surprisingly) we should look to our enemies for the most revealing reflection of ourselves. Such self-knowledge is essential "to secure to us the approbation of that being, to whom we are accountable for our thoughts and actions, and whose favour must finally constitute our total happiness" (3:151). Our goal is to "commune with our own hearts, and be still," to remove everything from our consideration "but God and ourselves" (3:157).

I think for Johnson the real difficulty of regulating our thoughts, our compositions, our lives, stems from the difficulty of being, as in this essay, "still"—focusing, as Paoli says to Boswell (in my epigraph), on "one great object" (Boswell 2:423n.1)—without diminishing our capacity to act. Unlike the incredible Paoli, we risk the paralysis of a deadly "neutrality" and despondency if we are not moving toward action, toward choice, toward "progeny." Perceiving the theoretical undecidability of even the most fundamental questions, Johnson recognizes the invigorating and expanding power of rigorous, open-ended analysis. But he also shuns the ultimately crippling effect in practice of deconstruction's final (and perhaps impossible) gesture, what Derrida calls "dissemination," in which opposing terms are dispersed, placed in question, written under erasure. Mr. Rambler cannot enjoy the total neutrality he claims and remain an undivided entity, just as he cannot retire completely and still exert his presence. We cannot retire and be "still" without remaining in the world and in motion. We cannot resolve the metaphysical disputes Paoli mentions to Boswell—fate or freedom, material or immaterial soul, matter or nonmatter (Boswell 2:423n.1)—but we also cannot "leave these disputes to the idle" either. Inevitably we are, Johnson suggests, the idle; and as Idlers and Ramblers and Adventurers we unavoidably encounter despondency. To "hold always one great object," as Paoli says he does, is for Johnson debilitating if not impossible. As *Rambler* 85 tells us, "nothing terrestrial can be kept at a stand": "Ease, if it is not rising into pleasure, will be falling towards pain," and "the vital powers unexcited by motion, grow gradually languid" (4:83).

Rambler 85 in fact offers a typical explanation of why "it is necessary to that perfection of which our present state is capable, that the mind and body should be kept in action," and "the faculties" not be allowed "to grow lax or torpid" (4:84). Johnson also deals here with the other sort of "faculties" who may even now at this moment be thinking of rowing machines and exercise bikes in closets gathering dust, for scholars, according to Johnson, are especially prone to physical inactivity, inevitably impairing their mental ability. Inactivity is debilitating even when it seems to be a state of ease, since "nothing terrestrial can be kept at a stand." Although *Rambler* 85 emphasizes the value of physical activity, even if it is only embroidering, its conclusion turns to the mental consequences of stasis: "It is certain that any wild wish or vain imagination never takes such firm possession of the mind, as when it is found empty and unoccupied" (4:86). This observation is true because the principle that "Nature abhors a Vacuum" applies to the intellect, "which will embrace any thing, however absurd or criminal, rather than be wholly without an object."

Four essays later, in *Rambler* 89, Johnson reverses the emphasis, glancing at "the exercises which the health of the body requires" (4:108) and concentrating on the psychological dangers. The impossibility of always engaging the mind in "profound study and intense meditation" will unavoidably involve us in some "trifles" (4:105). It is therefore crucial—it is the "great resolution" even—"that no part of life be spent in a state of neutrality or indifference; but that some pleasure be found for every moment that is not devoted to labour" (4:107–8). As his own life amply illustrated, Johnson recommends conversation, "the gay contention for paradoxical positions" that may "give new light to the mind" and "rectify the opinions" (4:108). Without this "gay" opposition, we are exposed to the "invisible riot of the mind" (4:106), and find ourselves "regulating the past, or planning out the future" (4:105), an "infatuation" that Johnson compares to "the poison of opiates" (4:106).

Of course conversation is not always possible, and it is therefore fortunate that we are not made to float placidly on the stream of time. "Providence has made the human soul an active being" (4:55)—a Rambler in other words. Yet we must always remember, as the essay on procrastination (*Rambler* 134) points out, how "we every day see the progress of life retarded by the *vis inertiae,* the mere repugnance to motion," even though "to act is far easier than to suffer" (4:347). There are many reasons for such a perversion of our fortunate imperfection, causing us to "freeze in idleness" or sink into sensual indulgence, but the bottom line is that "idleness never can secure tranquillity" (4:348), in life or in letters. Even Tranquilla cannot secure tranquillity, but her complementary marriage to Hymenaeus is a move in that direction. Another danger, as we have seen in other essays, is the possibility of "many objects of persuit" arising "at the same time." Once again Johnson's elaboration of this problem may well sound to some twentieth-century readers like the perfect image of a deconstructor hoisted on his own petard. "He whose penetration extends to remote consequences," who in any design "discovers new prospects of advantage, and possibilities of improvement," may easily "superadd one contrivance to another, endeavour to unite various purposes in one operation, multiply complications, and refine niceties, till he is entangled in his scheme, and bewildered in the complexity of various intentions" (4:349). Whether this "roving to no purpose," losing "the opportunity of doing well," actually describes Derrida or de Man, it certainly pertains to all ramblers, including "the Rambler," who found himself, according to the opening of *Rambler* 134, "awakened" from a "dream of study by a summons from the press" (4:345), which forced him to write what we are reading (and probably, we must admit, daydreaming) through.

The solution, as this maligned essay on procrastination eloquently articulates and demonstrates, is to "awaken" to whatever it is we are doing, which on the face of it should not be particularly difficult since "it is indeed natural to have particular regard to the time present" (4:346). We may not be made for this world, but we are made to move (or ramble) through it, working at pleasure, playing at work. Aspiring to awaken, as we have seen, is a recurrent idea. In *Rambler* 29 Johnson calls it "the secure possession of the present moment" (3:158), avoiding a mindless idleness, yet avoiding also being absorbed in present sensations. Possess yet do not be possessed; be still but not idle. The problem, the reason that

208 challenging essays can only begin to address this challenge, is that we are being directed to do the very thing our nature seems to drive us toward yet at the same time to make all but impossible. We keep chasing after tranquillity yet we are designed for discontent, and "something is always wanting to happiness," Johnson tells us (once more) even after 195 interrelated essays (5:261).

Although Johnson's readers have occasionally noted how some few essays not explicitly connected seem to be linked, John Worden's dissertation provides the most ambitious grouping, identifying some fifty-two essays that fall into twenty different clusters. For instance, Worden says that *Ramblers* 183 through 187 deal with the idea that "pain caused by life's inequalities" is "more imaginary than real" (187). Such associations greatly simplify the essays, but I think that the foregoing analysis, which could be expanded easily, suggests that Worden is on a productive track.

James Boyd White for instance cites *Rambler* 183, "written against envy," which "concludes with the statement that one may even enlist one's pride against this vice, a judgment that would surprise the reader of number 185, which inveighs in the strongest possible terms against pride" (152). The intervening essay, *Rambler* 184, as we shall see in detail shortly, tacitly connects the two by seeking to limit the domain of any pride we might marshall against envy, for "nothing that has life for its basis, can boast much stability" (4:204), and our nearly helpless state thus hardly warrants pride. *Rambler* 185 builds on this idea, arguing that our ignorance and impotence, dramatically presented in the preceding essay, necessitate the "speedy forgiveness" of our enemies (5:209). We "know not to what degree of malignity any injury is to be imputed; or how much its guilt, if we were to inspect the mind of him that committed it, would be extenuated by mistake, precipitance, or negligence" (5:208–9). *Rambler* 184 questions whether we can control, or whether any One controls our lives, and it concludes that for our well-being we must choose to believe in choice. *Rambler* 185 is similarly concerned with control, observing that pride can lead us "to resign the right of directing our own lives" (5:209). If we can control nothing else, we can always forgive, an act of surprising power: as this Christmas Eve essay appropriately reminds us, "on this great duty eternity is suspended, and to him that refuses to practice it, the throne of mercy is inaccessible, and the Saviour of the world has been born in vain" (5:210).

Thus, where White sees *Ramblers* 183 and 185 as "apparently incompatible or inconsistent," which he takes as evidence that every essay "begins afresh in the world of ordinary language and moves in its own direction" (152), I see these two essays and *Rambler* 184 as well working in concert to affect Johnson's reader, complementing and qualifying each other, providing subsequent and supplementary views leading to a declaration of faith.

Therefore, what Bate says of the whole of Johnson's moral writings—"Hardly any theme is single in Johnson," as "it is always being subsumed within a larger harmony" (*Achievement* 137)—is especially true for *The Rambler*. But in considering the resonances, echoes, and contrapuntal harmonies, at what point do we stop? If, as White claims, Johnson can write *Rambler* 175, supporting a prudent mistrust, to balance *Rambler* 79, which advises us "not to suppress tenderness by suspicion" (152), then we may be underrating Johnson's work (or ourselves) if we do not indulge in the ingenuity needed to see it in its entirety as a concerted whole, a single symphony.

"And Enquire How He Was Placed"

At this point I want to move from the relationship of various essays to the question of how the essays themselves are constructed and correspondingly shape our response. It will be useful here to consider briefly the historical context of ideas about writing and its production. An impressive number of valuable studies have noted Johnson's Lockean empiricism and skepticism, emphasizing his awareness and endorsement of the methodology of the new science.[7] If Johnson's methodology is in fact based upon associative reasoning, inductive investigation, and inferential proof, then the form of his discourse quite naturally would reflect the shift in eighteenth-century rhetorical theories from persuasion to discovery, from Aristotelian structures to Lockean procedures, from rituals of arrangement to operations of inquiry and invention.[8] This shift in rhetorical theory nicely parallels a contemporaneous shift in literary criticism documented by M. H. Abrams, from a "pragmatic" criticism evaluating works in terms of their effects to an "expressive" criticism evaluating works in terms of the writer's inspiration and insight (*Mirror* 14–26).

The next logical step would appear to be linking Johnson's writing (his process and his product) to Lockean epistemology, the new rhetoric, and an emerging romantic criticism. Resistance to this satisfyingly expansive view of Johnson in his time is, however, easy to find. Johnson endorses a handful of the new rhetoricians (Watts, Duncan, Le Clerc, Wolfius, Crousaz) in his preface to Dodsley's *Preceptor* (1748), his most extensive statement on rhetorical theory, published two years before the start of *The Rambler*. But he also recommends Aristotle and his modern followers, Sanderson, Wallis, and Crackenthorpe (Hazen 185).[9] In addition to this split allegiance, Johnson's declared aims both in generating and evaluating writing are not the intentions privileged in the new rhetoric or the new criticism. In the "Preface to Shakespeare" Johnson declares "the end of writing is to instruct; the end of poetry is to instruct by pleasing" (*Johnson on Shakespeare* 7:67). In *Rambler* 3, he announces that "the task of an author is, either to teach what is not known, or to recommend known truths" (3:14–15). Shortly thereafter, in number 8, he describes his "purpose" as "the moral discipline of the mind" and "the increase of virtue rather than learning" (3:42). Three essays later, in number 11, Johnson declares his "chief end" is "the regulation of common life" (3:57). In his private journal he prays for guidance in the *Rambler* in promoting "the Salvation both of myself and others" (*Diaries* 1:43). In the *Life of Dryden* he writes, "It is not by comparing line with line that the merit of great works is to be estimated, but by their general effects and ultimate result" (*Lives* 1:454).[10]

Still, although Johnson may not in his theoretical remarks sound like a critic or writer oriented toward inspiration, inquiry, and inference, what does the practice of his writing actually tell us? Do Johnson's textual structures reflect his process of exploratory thinking rather than a product designed to affect readers? It depends, of course, on how one reads. I argue that Johnson ultimately wants to convey the truth to readers in a process of (re)discovery, not merely to discover it for himself, and so his essays exhibit both the shape of discovery and presentation. To clarify this point, I turn briefly to an overview of the distinctive features of the traditional, Aristotelian/Ciceronian rhetoric versus the new, Lockean/scientific rhetoric.[11]

The old rhetoric concentrates on persuasion, whereas the new rhetoric, partly in response to the needs of science, encompasses broader aims that include conveying information and investigating truth. While the old rhetoric advocates beginning with commonplaces that are subjected to deductive manipulation, the new rhetoric grounds discourse upon experience and inferential reasoning: proof derived from authorities and words, versus truth derived from reality and individual reasoning. The old rhetoric offers the writer a formulaic arrangement, but in the new rhetoric *dispositio* follows the flow of thought (presentational versus investigative procedures again). In terms of the ancient struggle over style, the grand style is valued by the old rhetoric, the plain style by the new. In the old rhetoric disputation is seen as a way to truth; in the new rhetoric disputation only sharpens one's ability to dispute, going nowhere. Thus, while the old rhetoric considers the *topoi* useful, the new rhetoric consults facts, not a set of commonplaces. In sum, the old rhetoric sees truth as equal to verbal consistency, and the new rhetoric recognizes a gap between words and things.

In the case of the *Rambler*, however, this neat dichotomy is misleading, for at mid-century no one had fully worked out the implications for rhetoric of Locke and the new science. Isaac Watts and William Duncan, the theorists Johnson appears to have admired and recommended most, certainly moved beyond the Aristotelianism of, say, John Sargeant or Dean Aldrich, but both remain clearly transitional figures.[12] Thus, where Johnson's practice agrees with Watts, Duncan, or other progressive rhetorical theorists, it is not necessarily in line with the Lockean rhetoric as it would variously emerge in the work of Blair, Whately, Campbell, Genung, and others.

Take the crucial question of starting points. Watts advises the writer to begin, in both inquiry and presentation (for the two activities begin to blend together), with "those things which are best known and most obvious" (*Logick* 351), and Duncan similarly instructs us to begin with self-evident truths (123). The antiquity of such an approach, obviously counter to the new rhetoric, can be traced back through classical rhetoric even to the second-century writing exercises of Hermogenes in which the student begins with some well-known proverb or saying.[13] Johnson always begins a *Rambler* with an epigraph drawn from the classics that functions much like a sermon text, encapsulating, stimulating, and authorizing what follows. In the "professedly serious" essays, which predominate in the series, and which are invariably the kind of essay cited in discussions of Johnson's structuring,[14] Johnson proceeds from the epigraph with an extension of what is "best known" by presenting in essay after essay an authoritative proposition in the opening sentences. The authority may be specified (Tully, Boileau, Celsus, Hesiod, Locke, Quintilian, Quintus Curtius), generalized ("many writers," "the politicians," "the writers"), or implied ("It is allowed that . . ."; "Corporal sensation is known to depend . . ."; "No complaint has been more frequently repeated in all ages than that . . .").

In these deliberative essays Johnson typically first clarifies his opening assertion, a maneuver that is certainly common sense and is also consistent with the advice of Duncan, Watts, and even Hermogenes. Watts, for example, advises the writer to make sure not only that his "fundamental propositions" are "evident and true" but also that they are "a little familiar to the mind, by dwelling upon them before you proceed farther."[15] Such a procedure, obviously consistent with traditional rhetoric's stance that truth is manipulated from true statements (which one needs to understand fully to manipulate effectively), can be illustrated by *Rambler* 166, which offers a typical opening. After an epigraph from Martial, translated in later editions of the *Rambler* as "Once poor, still poor you must

remain, / The rich alone have all the means of gain," the essay
begins this way (I have arranged and numbered the text):

1. No complaint has been more frequently repeated in all ages than
   a that of neglect of merit associated with poverty, and
   b the difficulty with which valuable or pleasing qualities force
      themselves into view, when they are obscured by indigence.
2. It has been long observed
   c that native beauty has little power to charm without the orna-
      ments which fortune bestows, and
   d that to want the favour of others is often sufficient to hinder
      us from obtaining it. (5:116)

The numbered propositions point to the authority of the idea stated
in *a*, that merit plus poverty leads to neglect. In *b*, *c*, and *d*, Johnson
"dwells" upon" his "fundamental proposition," embellishing it
with submerged allegories in *b* and *c*, restating it in *d* in a kind of
catch–22 maxim.

Johnson's procedure at this point characteristically takes his
method beyond the traditional rhetoric into the transitional ground
(moving toward the new rhetoric) one finds occupied by Watts,
Duncan, and other Lockeans until well after mid-century. As Hoyt
Trowbridge notes, "Locke emphatically and repeatedly warns
against the dangers of regulating our assent entirely by the opinions
of others" (15). Having dwelled on the opinions of others, Johnson
moves to examine his starting point "on all sides with the utmost
Accuracy," as Watts for example advises. The grounds for testing
an assertion, the grounds of probability, are only two in Locke:
"The conformity of anything with our knowledge, observation, and
experience"; and secondly, "The testimony of others vouching their
observation and experience" (656). Again and again we see Johnson
testing a proposition in the *Rambler* not by its intuitive acceptability
or syllogistic potential but rather by its congruence with empirical
data. In terms of Kuhn's model of scientific discovery, Johnson
characteristically proceeds toward epistemological change, in the
fashion of the new science, by testing established dogma against
observation of facts. Although Johnson's method of beginning ties

him to the old logic of words, his manner of proceeding links him to the emerging logic of things.

In this testing move, Johnson may well confirm the proposition, as in *Rambler* 179 ("Every hour furnishes some confirmation of Tully's precept"), or he may qualify or even reject it, as in *Rambler* 168 ("every man . . . perceives" by reference to his own experience that Boileau's proposition, which opens the essay, will not hold up). Johnson's recourse to reality, to his own experience and observation, also oddly enough often employs analogy, a tactic important in Locke's account of probability (666), as a kind of test. In *Rambler* 173 he reasons: "Any action or posture long continued, will distort and disfigure the limbs; so the mind is likewise crippled and contracted by perpetual application to the same set of ideas" (5:150). Johnson's testing, especially his analogical testing, is only vaguely scientific. Yet his movement toward the orientation of the new science and empirical evidence can be suggested by his characteristic choice of analogues from mechanical and scientific fields. W. K. Wimsatt has said that the *Rambler* essays "exhibit perhaps the most concentrated use in English literature of mechanical imagery turned inward to the analysis of the soul" (*Philosophic Words* 32).[16] For Johnson, the mechanisms of the limbs and muscles constitute empirical data against which one can test the working of the mind.

The use to which Johnson puts the foregoing steps—epigraph, authoritative proposition, elaboration, and test—often appears on the surface to be complicated, unpredictable, myriad. Johnson's style, aligned with the old rhetoric's appreciation for the grand style, obviously does not help reveal recurrent maneuvers. But when one analyzes whole essays carefully for their possible rhetorical arrangement, moving back from the syntactic surface, patterns begin to emerge. The surface complexity is designed to obscure these recurrent organizational patterns. Johnson repeatedly stresses the value of novelty and in *Rambler* 143 reveals his acute awareness of "a common stock of images, a settled mode of arrangement, and a beaten track of transition" from which all writers must draw (4:394). It is also designed to demand the reader's energetic engagement with the text. If the *Rambler* is designed to save men's souls, it must first have their committed attention. In effect, the overall organizing patterns of individual *Rambler* essays are logically superior to the connections. My contention is that Johnson's essays rely on certain paradigms or structural formulas, and the formulas are holistic, not connective; rhetorical and not investigative. In fact, I find that Johnson often neglects to make explicit transitions, forcing the reader to supply the relationship—to see the part in terms of the whole.

Johnson uses what I will call an "application" section to proceed beyond testing the opening proposition. Three strategies in this application section seem immediately obvious and frequently recurrent. First is an illative sequence, in which the essay proceeds in a chain of "therefore" relationships. Next is a motivational sequence, in which Johnson explains why people behave the way they do—in other words, why the tested proposition has its particular status. And finally there is a crucial complementary pattern, in which Johnson's procedure, much like his conversational tactics, is to play one point against its counterpoint. The first of these maneuvers might be seen as Aristotelian; the second is perhaps more Lockean and scientific; and the third appears in some ways in tune with the old rhetoric's faith in disputation—although the way Johnson uses this back-and-forth movement might also be called deconstructive. The three maneuvers are often at work together, and I would like to show how this application step works and further clarify the underlying structure Johnson is using by analyzing some particular essays, beginning with what is in many ways a typical one, *Rambler* 172.

Johnson's opening paragraph in *Rambler* 172, like *Rambler* 166, has three elements. He begins with a proposition, echoing his epigraph from Martial, that "a change of fortune causes a change of manners." He then asserts the authority of the proposition, in two phrases, "nothing has been longer observed" and "it is generally agreed." And next comes an elaboration that narrows and specifies the starting proposition, telling us that a change in fortune for the better generally causes a change in manners for the worse, a point illustrated by a botanical comparison (in "the sun-shine of felicity," Johnson says, men "more frequently luxuriate into follies than blossom into goodness").

143

Johnson tests this proposition against experience and quickly confirms it. "Many observations have concurred to establish this opinion, and it is not likely soon to become obsolete, for want of new occasions to revive it" (5:146). In "applying" the confirmed proposition, Johnson first examines the motives underlying its truth. Yet, in explaining why riches corrupt, Johnson appears to open up the possibility that riches in themselves do not really corrupt, but rather that men are corrupt to begin with—money merely empowers their evil—and they often become more evil in the act of acquiring money, not necessarily possessing it. Johnson's next move, opening the third paragraph, develops this emerging counterpoint, asserting "that the deprivation of the mind by external advantages, though certainly not uncommon, yet approaches not so nearly to universality as some have asserted." The reason is because it is only natural for us to envy those who have risen above us. Johnson concludes this line of thought at the end of the fifth paragraph: "Riches therefore do not so often produce crimes as incite accusers" (5:147). The first half of paragraph six, however, reverts to the analysis of motives and counters in fact the fifth paragraph's strong closing by supporting once again the common charge that the wealthy are vain. The corruption of the wealthy may be qualified, but we must nonetheless admit their pride—because it is all too human to "rate ourselves by our fortune rather than our virtues." And yet, in the last half of this same sixth paragraph, Johnson once again immediately complicates and counters his preceding point, this time observing that, still, "captiousness and jealousy are easily offended," an observation in which the pride of the wealthy is eclipsed by the vanity of the observer (who termed the wealthy vain).

Just when we may be believing that the opening proposition is about to collapse, paragraph seven confronts us with yet another counterpoint in its support, beginning, "It must however be confessed that as all sudden changes are dangerous, a quick transition from poverty to abundance, can seldom be made with safety." This and the two subsequent paragraphs sharpen and confirm the assertion under debate. We find that yes, it is after all true that sudden wealth corrupts. Sudden wealth corrupts because of the overwhelming and universal power of novelty, a familiar theme in the series. Every reader of this paper, Johnson says, has been at some point "overpowered by the transitory charms of trifling novelty" (5:148).

Thus, we have seen that wealth corrupts because "the greater part of mankind are corrupt in every condition," because the rich display the same pride anyone would exhibit in the same circumstances, and because novelty, which overpowers all of us in trivial things, easily and quite naturally overwhelms the suddenly rich. In the countering movements we have also seen that in asserting the corruption of the wealthy one vitiates oneself. The accused are significantly defended; the accusers are significantly implicated.

Given this progressive dissolution of the categories of corrupt, wealthy, vain, observer, and innocent, which at least approximates a deconstructive movement, the beginning of paragraph ten, which stands in an unstated "therefore" relationship to the foregoing essay, seems well prepared. "Some indulgence is due to him whom a happy gale of fortune has suddenly transported into new regions, where unaccustomed lustre dazzles his eyes and untasted delicacies solicit his appetite" (5:148–49). We ought therefore to alleviate our censures of the powerful and the rich because they lack objective advisers, being surrounded by flattering sycophants, and because "virtue is sufficiently difficult with any circumstances" (5:150). We have been moved into a position from which it is virtually impossible to judge others. Thus Johnson moves into what I would term "the call," the typical closing maneuver in his deliberative essays, turning our attention to our own status. Again and again, with varying degrees of subtlety, Johnson in closing an essay calls the reader to action: to moral discipline, to regulation of the mind—in this case, to sympathy and vigilance. Although these essays exist for the sake of the closing directive, Johnson's "calls" are typically as unemphatic as this one. Johnson's subtlety is possible and effective because of his structuring of the reader's experience. We have come to understand how difficult virtue is "with any circumstances," and why "some indulgence is due" to those who have become wealthy.

145

Johnson's method in this essay and many others is hardly in the final analysis deductive or inductive, Aristotelian or Lockean, although it draws from both. Johnson establishes a proposition and then, seemingly extending Watts's advice to examine starting propositions on all sides, he dismantles his starting point, teasing out its contradictions, its omissions, its difference from itself. His use of what I have termed the epigraph, authoritative proposition, elaboration, test, application, and call, does not seem spontaneous or exploratory or ad hoc or associative or illogical or Shandean. It appears to be a formulaic procedure, in the tradition of Aristotle that involves rigorous empirical analysis, in the tradition of Locke and the new science—but that seems in the final analysis committed to the sort of rigorous thinking through that marks deconstruction.

In order to give some indication that *Rambler* 172 is not idiosyncratic and also to suggest the flexibility (as well as the existence) of the paradigm I am positing, it seems wise to examine other essays in some detail. *Rambler* 184 is a good choice. For one thing, this essay has been seen as a classic example of Johnson's exploratory structures and haphazard composing strategies. In *Rambler* 184, says Fussell, Johnson offers one example after another of "the dominion of chance" only to realize "where he has been led." Because he cannot acknowledge that chance governs all, Johnson is forced, Fussell remarks, to abandon what he has written, tack on a pious ending, and hope the reader will not notice (164). Or, as O'Flaherty puts it, in *Rambler* 184 we see Johnson "sacrificing logical consistency for what he believes is the truth," displaying "an utter disregard for his own conclusions when they foolishly contradict what has been ordained" (535). These readings fulfill certain expectations about Johnson's composing process, his insight, and his faith. After deconstruction, other readings are always possible— supplements are always possible. What is missing from O'Flaherty's and Fussell's readings is the alternative assumption that Johnson knew what he doing, that his pious ending is tacked on as a consequence of his reasoning, that Johnson employs the appearance of pervasive arbitrariness, and that his essay implies we ought always (given the nature of language and logic) to abandon what we have written in favor of pious endings.

146

In opening *Rambler* 184 Johnson asserts that writing is in some respects like life: "As every scheme of life, so every form of writing has its advantages and inconveniences" (5:201). This proposition is presented as a given; it is an authoritative, accepted idea (a Johnsonian commonplace, we might say, but also an idea pervasive in his age). Johnson will "dwell upon" this generalization, and at the same time confirm its validity (the test stage) with extended examples. Although essayists, we learn, escape "long trains of consequence," lengthy and mind-numbing "perusal of antiquated volumes," and "great accumulations of preparatory knowledge," even so they are "distressed" by "the perpetual demand of novelty and change" (5:201). Writers in other genres face different problems but a similar mix of advantages and inconveniences. The "compiler of science" or "the relator of feigned adventures," for instance, struggles to find a "seminal idea" or to establish characters and events, but once this task is accomplished he "lays his invention at rest" as "the latter part . . . grows without labour out of the former" (5:201). The essayist's particular challenge of "novelty and change" might seem insignificant in comparison, Johnson acknowledges, since almost any topic would seem suitable for an essay. In reality, however, "it often happens that the judgment is distracted with boundless multiplicity, the imagination ranges from one design to another," until the harried essayist, pressed by his deadline, is forced to employ whatever ideas "then happen to be at hand" (5:202). Thus the writer who would appear the least constrained, the essayist, is often tyrannized by his obligation to choose, even though he is "without any principle to regulate his choice" (5:202). The outcome of such arbitrary points of departure, surprisingly enough, is often fortunate, as "the mind, rejoicing at deliverance on any terms from perplexity and suspense, applies herself vigorously to the work before her, collects embellishments and illustrations, and sometimes finishes with great elegance and happiness what in a state of ease and leisure she never had begun" (5:202). Thus, while the essayist's expansive freedom tends to overwhelm and paralyze him, the confines of a deadline and an enforced arbitrary decision liberate and determine his beginning.

In other words, in *Rambler* 184 Johnson characteristically engages in a deconstructive complication of alternative concepts that must give way to choice (to progeny) or lapse into paralysis. To put it yet another way, Johnson appears to grasp Derrida's final deconstructive gesture, dissemination, in which opposing terms are placed in question, under erasure, in suspension; or at least Johnson has a profound sense of the undecidability of even fundamental questions. And yet he moves through deconstruction, using his rigorous analyses and reversals to reveal more fully the shifting ground on which he chooses, exposing our place within life's "maze" or "labyrinth," or on life's open sea, to use three of Johnson's favorite images. We must avoid extremes, Johnson tells us, and avoid getting stuck in the middle. The "composition" of our self, which as Johnson says ideally emerges from playing body against mind, is related to the composition of an essay as we regulate one part by some regard to the other.

Having exposed the contradictory nature of writing, Johnson returns to his opening analogy, which compared life to writing, and enters the "application" section of his essay. He notes that the role of "accident, or some cause out of our own power" is not limited to writing and then drives home this observation by having (as he often does) the reader inventory his own experience: "Let him that peruses this paper, review the series of his life, and enquire how he was placed in his present position" (5:202). In this pivotal sentence, the reader's volitional actions—pursuing, reviewing, inquiring—are confronted alliteratively (peruse/paper), metaphorically (review/the *series* of life), and semantically ("enquire"—a willed seeking, from *quaerere*/how he was *placed*—an absence of will) by that which is beyond his control, just as his living and inquiring (again, supposedly under his direction) vanish into his life (a product of forces largely beyond his control, a "series" into which one happens to be placed). Such a review reveals most emphatically our ignorance about how we were placed here in this essay series or in life's series of essays—or for that matter where here is in any significant sense. Language and life take us where we do not know.

From this transition, writing to living, Johnson moves to consider various schemes for behavior. This consideration is tacitly structured by the notion of authorial control—the same organizing principle silently used to analyze genres of writing in the essay's movement from proposition to elaboration to test sequence, thus further tightening the analogy between living and writing. Those who would seem to have the least control, "the busy, the ambitious, the inconstant, and the adventurous," appear "to throw themselves by design into the arms of fortune, and voluntarily to quit the power of governing themselves" (5:202). In other words, those with the least control are the most constrained or governed from without. In opposition to these reckless folk, Johnson presents those persons who control themselves the most, "timorous" persons who "make no step till they think themselves secure from the hazard of a precipice." Johnson's spectra for forms of writing and schemes for living allow him in both instances to isolate the extreme and therefore most convincing examples: essayists who are constricted and thus liberated by a deadline, and scientists or storytellers whose unbounded imaginations bind the development of any work; the fearless, who exercise their will in order to abandon it, and the fearful, who retain their will only by paralyzing it. This inquiry into human motivation is characteristically brought to an illative application. We may conclude that just as no form of writing (not even the essay) escapes "the dominion of chance," by the same token no course of life (not even the most "prescribed and limited") can escape the fact that "many actions must result from arbitrary election" (5:203). Even under the most favorable conditions, in writing as in living, human control is effectively erased by chance, subjecting us to advantages and conveniences regardless of our own efforts.

Thus in the first part of *Rambler* 184 an essay writer examines essay writing, and in the second part Johnson exhorts the readers to "read" their own lives. Such a double reflection, far from being the accidental remains of exploratory connection and syntactic manipulation, appears in fact immanent in the essay's opening comparison of life and writing.

Even so, although the movement of this essay seems far from exploratory, ad hoc, or Shandean, its design at this point appears possibly to have been incomplete (Johnson does discuss the writer

149

who is caught by his deadline). Despite its control thus far the essay seems inexorably, uncontrollably we might say, to be leading with Johnsonian force toward a very unsettling view—a view that in fact is presented in the opening of the penultimate paragraph: "Since life itself is uncertain, nothing which has life for its basis, can boast much stability" (5:204). As if this observation were not bleak enough, the next sentence continues, "Yet this is but a small part of our perplexity," a point which is underscored by the immediate translation of our perplexity into nautical dangers—"a tempestous sea," "cross winds," meteors, and deadly whirlpools, all of which randomly threaten us, often unseen, at every moment (5:204–5).

Surely Johnson's muse, his syntactic manipulation, and his spontaneous writing have all led him, as modern critics have observed, to the edge of a rhetorical cliff where he must either jump off, sit down, or walk back. Johnson must either admit that chance rules our meaningless lives, or drop the topic and end the essay, or deny the logical thrust of what he has written. So it appears. This is by no means the first apparent endpoint of undecidability, followed by a decision, that Johnson's reader has encountered. Indeed, the series begins by demonstrating the impossibility of deciding how to begin.

Only by quoting the entire final paragraph can one begin to suggest the extent to which the conclusion of this essay is the strategical culmination of a carefully designed rhetorical tour de force:

> In this state of universal uncertainty, where a thousand dangers hover about us, and none can tell whether the next step will lead him to safety or destruction, nothing can afford any rational tranquility, but the conviction that, however we amuse ourselves with unideal sounds, nothing in reality is governed by chance, but that the universe is under the perpetual superintendence of him who created it; that our being is in the hands of omnipotent goodness, by whom what appears casual to us is directed for ends ultimately kind and merciful; and that nothing can finally hurt him who debars not himself from divine favour. (5:205)

We see Johnson asserting here that it is the very appearance of uncertainty and chance which logically necessitates that we believe "nothing in reality is governed by chance": nothing else "can afford any rational tranquility." This startling conclusion, his "call" as I have termed it, is in fact far from being a "wholly new direction" or a disconnected appendage. Such Möbius-strip logic, by which one thing turns mysteriously into its opposite without disjunction, has in fact permeated the essay. This strategy is what I referred to as a complementary or even deconstructive movement in *Rambler* 172. By progressively collapsing any faith we might have in things of this world, Johnson has hoped to prepare the reader, made intensely uneasy by the exposure of his impotence and vulnerability, to grasp at the other-worldly stability—the only real stability—held out in this final paragraph. (In *Rambler* 172 Johnson similarly dismantled the categories of "wealthy," "accuser," "corrupt," in order to urge the reader toward diligence and tolerance.) The ending of *Rambler* 184 is prepared for early in the essay, in the fourth paragraph, for example, when he says that many events seem to be "*influenced by causes* acting without [our] intervening," and that actions appear to result from "accident, or *some cause out of our power*, by whatever name it be distinguished" (5:202–3; emphasis added). These statements, which may have appeared at first sight to support the rule of chance, turn out in retrospect to point like all the other evidence to the absence of chance—when correctly read. Johnson's closing paragraph identifies the "cause out of our power" and the "causes acting without our intervening" as "the hands of omnipotent goodness." Just as our experience of the essay finally exposes the hidden control of its author, so we may believe our experience of life will ultimately reveal the unseen but "perpetual superintendence" of its Author.

This movement is indeed immanent in the essay's epigraph, its real starting point, which is taken from Juvenal's *Tenth Satire*—the poem that is of course the basis for *The Vanity of Human Wishes*. Clearly this sentiment is important for Johnson:

> *Permittes ipsis expendere numinibus, quid*
> *Conveniat nobis, rebusque sit utile nostris.*   (5:200)

Samuel Johnson after Deconstruction

Here is Dryden's translation:

> *Intrust thy fortune to the pow'rs above:*
> *Leave them to manage for thee, and to grant*
> *What their unerring wisdom sees thee want.* (5:201)

From a pagan satirist, Johnson develops the essay's religious directive; from the pervasiveness of chance, he draws out the necessity of faith.

Johnson's strategy in this carefully crafted essay (like that in *Rambler* 172), which is admittedly quite stunning, is quite similar to his tactics elsewhere. We might glance briefly at *Rambler* 155, which has heretofore been viewed as an "associative" essay, an instance of a writing practice which "sometimes—perhaps often" results in "a miscellany or hodge-podge rather than a unified series of reflections" (Damrosch, "Johnson's Manner" 84). The *dispositio* of this essay is very far from a hodge-podge. Johnson focuses, as in *Ramblers* 172, 184, and many others, on a familiar notion—in this case, "the negligence with which men overlook their own faults, however flagrant." In a tightly orchestrated dialectic, Johnson scrutinizes his starting point, the postulate that we simply cannot see our own faults, "as the eye cannot see itself," a notion that Johnson shows would explain a great deal. However, taking the other side, Johnson moves on to assert that in reality "self-love is often rather arrogant than blind; it does not hide our faults from ourselves, but persuades us that they escape the notice of others" (5:60). But, on the other hand, countering his counterpoint, "the most absurd and incredible flattery" seems consistently to be accepted (5:61). One might therefore suspect that we are often ignorant of ourselves. Johnson continues his complementary analysis of human motivation, once again exposing the gap in the preceding conclusion, asserting that flattery, "if its operation be nearly examined, will be found to owe its acceptance not to our ignorance but knowledge of our failures." Because we acutely know our shortcomings, we are especially pleased to find that others have missed them. Yet Johnson once again raises the supplementary point, wondering why, if we know our own faults, advice is so often ignored. Not because,

152

as one might first think, we do not know ourselves, but "because [the advice] shows that we are known to others as well as to ourselves," thus earning our resentment and embarrassed disregard (5:61). Having teased out of his opening proposition its own antithesis, Johnson concludes in paragraph eight that if we know ourselves so well, then every man must surely "intend some time to review his conduct, and to regulate the remainder of his life by the laws of virtue" (5:62–3).

From this proposition at the center of the *Rambler's* mission, Johnson continues not in "a wholly new direction"; rather, he moves deliberately to effect the essay's rhetorical purpose. If people know themselves and if they intend to reform, why then do they continue, as Johnson has said in this essay's first sentence, to "overlook their own faults, however flagrant"? Because "procrastination is accumulated on procrastination" (5:63). We know ourselves but put off the unpleasantness of confronting and acting upon that knowledge. As Johnson puts it in the final paragraph, thus (once again) bringing the reader to the edge of a decision to acknowledge his own faults and reform, "we all know our own state, if we could be induced to consider it" (5:65)—and there Johnson leaves the reader on the verge of considering his own (precarious) condition.

An armada of deliberative *Rambler* essays could be presented as proof of Johnson's recurrent, holistic, well-crafted, rhetorical *dispositio*. In fact, one might also argue that other kinds of *Ramblers* exhibit similar strategies. For example, *Ramblers* 204 and 205 comprise an oriental tale featuring Seged, who discovers (like Rasselas) the emptiness of having all his desires met. Seged mandates that he will devote ten days to happiness—only to be confronted repeatedly with "the uncertainty of human schemes" (5:296–305). Each time Seged devises a plan for happiness some unforeseen disturbance breaks in, until finally Seged, Lord of Ethiopia, emperor of riches, must consider his own state and acknowledge his impotence over dreams, crocodiles, illness, and the other things of this earth, which appears (yet again) to be ruled by chance. By severing man's attachment to this unreliable world, Johnson paves the way for trust in the only sphere—the eternal—which can afford "rational tranquility." In both the *Vanity of Human Wishes* and *Rasselas*, Johnson similarly eliminates one possible center of value and choice of life after another, thereby exposing the uncertainty of earthly things, before finally pointing to the necessity of indulgence, vigilance, and faith in eternity. But it is *The Rambler* that most powerfully and engagingly shows us how after deconstruction we may save the self, inevitably out of place here within language, by ceasing to believe in it and by believing in an Other elsewhere, creating our self-will by exercising it. *The Rambler* is, as Tetty said, his "pure wine," most sobering.

5

Conclusion:
"The Only Proper and
Adequate Relief"

. . . and suddenly there is no limit

To what a man can get out of
His failure to see.
—James Dickey, "Night Bird"

Of the many fascinating things about Samuel Johnson, one is certainly a list of the four poets inserted by his recommendation into the *Lives of the English Poets.* Passing over Marvell, Herrick, Lovelace, Churchill, Crashaw, Chatterton, and others, Johnson asks the publishers to add Thomas Yalden, Richard Blackmore, Isaac Watts, and John Pomfret (*Lives* 1:301). Perhaps Yalden is included because Johnson could not resist pointing out that two stanzas of his *Hymn to Darkness* seem to be taken from Wowerus's *Hymnus ad Umbram* (2:302), especially since Yalden at the outset of his career had won the favor of Magdalen College's president by clearing himself of a suspected plagiarism (2:297–98). Blackmore is probably included because he had been given "worse treatment than he deserved" (2:252). Watts is there perhaps because Johnson greatly admired his piety and versatility. And why choose Pomfret? His inclusion, it seems clear, depends on one brief poem, "The Choice," which Johnson praises in a whisper: it exhibits "a system of life adapted to common notions and equal to common expectations" (1:302), appealing to "that class of readers" who "seek only their own amusement." Yet Pomfret must be included because, as Johnson says in a statement startling to modern readers, "perhaps no composition in our language has been oftener perused than Pomfret's *Choice*" (1:302). "The Choice," Johnson recognizes, addresses in a thoroughly typical fashion a fundamental topic, perennially of interest but especially engaging to Johnson's century. In a familiar tradition of Horatian retirement poems, using the Aristotelian golden mean as his basic guiding principle, Pomfret outlines his ideal life.

Johnson's own lack of enthusiasm for the poem cannot be based on any lack of interest in the topic; for many reasons, he remained throughout his career intensely interested in "the choice of life" and the whole activity of choosing. Rather, Johnson's reaction to Pomfret's easy platitudes must be based in part on his characteristically skeptical attitude toward all idealistic visions. Although almost any number of Johnson's own works might have been called "The Choice of Life," the work that actually had that as its working title begins with "Ye who listen with credulity to the whispers of fancy, and persue with eagerness the phantoms of hope," and it goes on to direct such visionaries to "attend to the history of Rasselas, prince of Abissinia" (*Rasselas* 1). What Rasselas learns about visionary schemes is arguably what Pomfret himself learned—in a darkly comical fashion, in fact, that would fit rather well into Johnson's tale. Having declared in his poem "I'd have no wife," Pomfret found his clergical career obstructed by the "malicious interpretation" that he advocated "a mistress." Ironically, like "almost all other men who plan schemes of life," as Johnson says, Pomfret "had departed from his purpose" and was already married (1:301–2).

The proper response to the failures and deflections of our purposes, detailed throughout Johnson's canon, is certainly not to suspend all "schemes of life" and live like animals. Nor is the proper response, as Johnson also makes clear, simply to go on ceaselessly interrogating and exposing this or that possible matrix of choosing.

156

From time to time we must choose one thing or another. What Johnson brings to our attention is the foreknowledge that our choices will become different, departing inevitably from our purposes, no matter how we suspend or evaluate our commitment; and so we must always choose again. But Johnson also leads us to an understanding of this labyrinth of choosing that makes our always-different-from-themselves decisions important.

Of course one could argue that we do not need deconstruction to have formed this insight, but its particular significance for Johnson is illuminated, I think, by such a conjunction. So in concluding, I want to reconsider the role that deconstruction has played out. I would like in particular to anticipate one way of looking at what I have undertaken.

Motivated by my own desire to salvage and justify some sort of belief in a Transcendent Other, I have read that interest back into Johnson's *Rambler* to the exclusion of other concerns. I have read *The Rambler*, which appears to be concerned with many things, as a single-minded evangelical document, casting Johnson as a lay preacher out to win our souls for God. In this reductive misreading deconstruction has been conscripted as my accomplice, disarming the normative forces of genre and history that would otherwise restrict my movements. Able to violate these conventions, reading *The Rambler* differently, I have disagreed at/on one point or another with virtually every Johnsonian living and dead including at times the original Johnsonian himself. In positing such a unity and center, I have violated the very method I invoke.

Having thus turned myself in, I want to answer these charges in the hope my reader will consider more charitably my sentence(s). I have used deconstruction here; but, as I said at the outset, this is obviously not a fully deconstructive reading. Instead, situating Johnson (and myself) after deconstruction, my rhetorical position has encouraged and authorized a close and contrary reading of *The Rambler*, not only by helping to suspend certain limiting expectations but also by focusing on Johnson's strategies. The result, I think, is that the *Rambler* papers may be seen as richer, more complex, more interesting than we may have suspected.

Specifically, I have tried to show that *The Rambler* responds pervasively and strategically to *The Spectator*, as Johnson misreads his predecessor in a variety of overt and subtle ways. The more closely we attend to this construction of his literary fathers, the more fully Johnson's own achievement comes into view. Although Bloom's theory of an antagonistic intertextuality focuses our attention on this material, Bloom's conception of rhetoric as the art of defense overlooks Johnson's persuasive deployment of a differentiated stance, as Bloom's own misreading of Johnson suggests.

Thus, in examining the persuasive art of Johnson's rhetoric, I have concluded that his series has a coherent purpose, and this claim provides a context for reading particular essays and groups of essays. I have argued that reading essays as a series, in Johnson's ordering, is especially stimulating. In making this argument, it should be clear, I am not inhabiting New Criticism. In proposing that Johnson holds to the purpose outlined in his inaugural prayer, that he ultimately intends to spark our faith and to save our souls (and his own), I am not claiming that *The Rambler* has the aesthetic unity of a well-wrought urn. Johnson's goal requires diversion, digression, misdirection, covertness: his audience already knows in essence what they most need to hear—what they would be most likely to ignore or resist if more blatantly addressed. There is of course a certain convenience in arguing for a rhetorical coherence that can include strategic divergences. But the value of this assumption can only be determined by its effects, and I think I have been able to place much of the series in a new light, starting with Johnson's title, which is no longer an unfortunate or eccentric whim, but becomes a not-so-subtle theological comment on the meaning of life.

This meaning emerges from a process that after deconstruction seems quite familiar, appearing repeatedly in terms of unstable and arbitrary oppositions, divided by a recurring absence that pervades language, time, space, consciousness, gender, authorial voice, everything. From a rhetorical perspective we can see how after deconstruction individual essays and groups of essays expose this absence and our consequent yearning. This movement within essays has been seen as the errant result of Johnson's procrastination and haste, but I have offered an alternative view, showing how

Johnson uses certain recurrent strategies to position the reader on the edge of belief in something outside this nothing. Part of this positioning involves Johnson's use of Mr. Rambler and his correspondents in a self-reflexive drama, and I have tried to indicate the richness of Johnson's strategies in that regard. We can see, for example, how Mr. Rambler functions as a character, a rhetorical construct, a name for Johnson strategically withdrawn, and a neutral cipher.

How we get from the cycle of desire and the insight that we are not at home here, that we are ramblers, is perhaps (as I have claimed) amazing and mazing, but it is not illogical. Although deconstruction certainly has served as a ground for atheism, for resisting (as Barthes puts it) "God and his hypostases—reason, science, law" (146), this association is not necessary. I am not alone, as I have indicated, in thinking that deconstruction and belief are not mutually exclusive but may in fact be ultimate allies. In drawing this conclusion, however, I may appear to be using deconstruction to argue on behalf of logocentrism. And so, in at least two senses, I am. Derrida's clearest and most abbreviated explanation of the "method" of deconstruction describes three movements. One first identifies the binary oppositions of a particular discourse and its consequent hierarchy; then one reverses this hierarchy, making for instance the first come last, the rich poor, the meek bold; and one finally "disseminates" the oppositions, placing their formation in question, under erasure. The second step, Derrida cautions, cannot be passed over, for to "overlook this phase of overturning is to forget the conflictual and subordinating structure of opposition" (*Positions* 41). Without establishing this reversal, Derrida says, "one might proceed too quickly to a *neutralization* that *in practice* would leave the previous field untouched, leaving one no hold on the previous opposition, thereby preventing any means of *intervening* in the field effectively" (41). In this sense, then, I am striving to reverse the secularization of Johnson's thought, operating within the second movement that needs to be fully explored, bringing to the forefront the religious nature of *The Rambler* that has been subordinated to other themes: in short, affirming the Other in Johnson's discourse.

Samuel Johnson after Deconstruction

One may legitimately ask, I think, if the final movement of deconstruction is always possible or always necessary or always desirable. Derrida's own practice suggests not. In "The Laws of Reflection: Nelson Mandela, in Admiration," Derrida indicates that some oppositions must stand outside deconstruction. Of Mandela, Derrida writes: "He presents himself in his people, before the law. Before a law he rejects, beyond any doubt, but which he rejects in the name of a superior law, the very one he declares to admire and before which he agrees *to appear*" ("Laws" 15). It is this "superior law" that Mandela respects and that motivates him to imagine an Edenic origin when "there were no classes, no rich or poor, and no exploitation of man by man. All men were free and equal and this was the foundation of government" (qtd. in Derrida, "Laws" 24). Here is an origin and a hierarchy, a law above the law, that Derrida will exempt from dissemination. That is not to say that deconstruction in theory contradicts anti-racism, which in practice Derrida ignores. It does mean that deconstruction, "forever wavering and wandering" as Mark Taylor says (*Erring* 10), acting within language, must look elsewhere for affirmative beliefs. Derrida is quite willing, as Robert Magliola puts it, to "cross-out," but extremely reluctant to "cross-over" (54), to look outside the frame of deconstruction. But "the sign," Derrida insists, "is always a sign of the Fall" (*Grammatology* 283), which we may take to be a reminder of our errant nature, a caution against committing ourselves to knowledge, and also a theological letter.

In his own way and in his own time Johnson is, I think, as rigorous as Derrida, and equally reluctant to exempt propositions from scrutiny. The motto chosen for the *Rambler* as a whole, after all, is the same passage the Royal Society had taken as its motto, and it pledges Johnson to the same sort of unprejudiced scientific investigation it had generally espoused.

> *Nullius addictus jurare in verba magistri,*
> *Quo me cunque rapit tempestas deferor hospes.*
> Horace, *Epistles* 1.1.14–15

Even in this motto, however, there is a hint of the proposition Johnson risks taking ultimately on faith. Here is Robert Olson's

160

translation: "Not obligated to swear by any master's orders, I turn in for refuge wherever the tempest drives me" (xxv). Johnson's work repeatedly will drive us to the same "refuge" from the tempest of life that Johnson chose—namely, religious faith. But I want to reiterate that Johnson's reluctance to name this refuge too easily, too directly, too redundantly, shapes the series. Elsewhere Johnson is equally reluctant to invoke a term beyond analysis. In his *Thoughts on the Late Transactions in the Falkland Islands*, for instance, as John Burke points out, Johnson "remarkably for the eighteenth century" avoids "any reference to Divine Providence, and therefore any claim whatsoever that God favored the English over the other peoples of the earth." As Burke puts it, "Johnson was too wise to allow his countrymen to use God to justify ambition and greed" ("Falklands" 306). Even Elphinston's translation of the collected edition's motto, which was not part of the original Folio, the Edinburgh edition (1750–52), or the first collected edition (London, 1752), displaces the already disguised "refuge" in Horace, saying merely:

> *Sworn to no master's arbitrary sway,*
> *I range where-e'er occasion points the way.*   (3:1)

But if Johnson is reluctant to say precisely what we should believe, he is dedicated in *The Rambler* to placing us in that posture of submitting to the Law beyond the law, the Word beyond the word. That is where he begins, with his prayer and his motto, and where he ends, awaiting the "last reward" for his "labours" of "piety" (5:320). As he says in number 69, confronting the future— what Derrida has called "the terrifying form of monstrosity" that is "the future" after deconstruction (*Writing* 293)—faith is quite simply the only "proper and adequate" choice we ramblers have:

> Piety is the only proper and adequate relief of decaying man. He that grows old without religious hopes, as he declines into imbecility, and feels pains and sorrows incessantly crowding upon him, falls into a gulph of bottomless misery, in which every reflexion must plunge him deeper, and where he finds only new gradations of anguish, and precipices of horror. (5:367)

Notes
Works Cited
Index

Notes

1. Introduction: Johnson upon His Bedside, after Deconstruction

1. On the distribution of the series, see Wiles. On the place of *The Rambler* in Johnson's career, see Bate, *Johnson* (1975) 289–95, Clifford 71–87, and Greene, *Johnson* (1970) 139–46. Bond estimates the initial printing of *The Spectator* rose to about three thousand, but he also argues that contemporary reports of fourteen thousand and twenty thousand for some individual issues may be accurate (Addison 1:xx–xxviii).

2. For Johnson's opinion that some essays could be made better and were "too wordy," see Boswell 4:5 and 4:309. I participated in Keast's challenge at the University of Texas in 1979. Subsequent references to Boswell are to the *Life* unless noted otherwise.

3. This remark continues, "they are generally so repulsive that I cannot" (William Bowles, "To James Boswell," 4 November 1787; in Boswell, *Correspondence* 251). See also Boswell 2:226, and Piozzi 332.

4. See Culler 3–14 or Graff 226–43.

5. See also Fussell 144 and Hibbert 75.

6. Boswell employs a similar strategy of proof-by-association a few pages later when he reports Johnson's disclosure that his style had been formed upon that of Sir William Temple and Ephraim Chambers. Boswell informs us, again "certainly," that Johnson "was mistaken" (1:218–19). Rather than explain how he knows more about the formation of Johnson's style than Johnson, Boswell instead merely illustrates his assertion, telling us "their styles differ

as plain cloth and brocade." Before the reader can question Boswell's judgment, he goes even further, asserting that Temple also was mistaken in his ideas of where he got his style, thinking in "equally erroneous" fashion he "had formed his style upon Sandys's *View of the State of Religion*" (1:219). By claiming that one great mind, Temple, misunderstood his stylistic lineage, Boswell aims to deflect our resistance to the idea that another even greater thinker, Johnson, misunderstood his, thus allowing Boswell to assert obliquely a mastery of his materials and even his subject.

7. Boswell thought this concluding quotation "unnecessary" and the reference to "Celestial pow'rs" (which is Johnson's translation) "ill suited to Christianity" (*Life* 1:226).

2. (Mis)Reading *The Spectator*: *The Rambler* in Bloom

1. The intricacies of Bloom's "revisionary ratios" are laid out in *The Anxiety of Influence* and developed further in *A Map of Misreading*. I have found especially helpful the discussions of Bloom by Jay ("Father Figures"), Fite, Elam, Riddel, and De Bolla.

2. Bloom has said that "an Oedipal interpretation of poetic history" is "the usual misunderstanding that my own work provokes" (*Poetry* xx). This "misreading" is indeed so widespread and warranted by Bloom's discussion that I accept it.

3. This anecdote is part of Maxwell's "Collectanea," which Boswell publishes (2:116–33). The advice is in fact given to Glaucus, and Clarke's translation is substantially different: "Ut semper fortissime rem gererem, et superior virtute essem aliis." Cowper's translation: "That I should outstrip always all mankind / In worth and valour." See Boswell 2:129.

4. As Grundy says, "The theme of competitive struggle to excel holds such an important place in [Johnson's] writings that it is amazing to find it still awaiting adequate critical attention" (*Greatness* 102). Although Grundy's chapter entitled "Competition" (102–19) surveys this theme in the *Rambler* and elsewhere, she does not cover the relationship I discuss here between the *Spectator* and the *Rambler*. On Johnson's view of conversation as a contest, see

especially Boswell 2:450, 3:80, 4:111. For resolutions to do more, see Johnson's *Diaries* 71, 73, 82, 110, 147, 155, 160, 268, 303.

5. All translations are my own unless noted otherwise. I have consulted, whenever possible, Olson and the appropriate Loeb volume.

6. "Poems are refusals of mortality," Bloom says (*Map* 19). See also, for example, *Kabbalah* 52 and *Anxiety* 10.

7. Richardson wrote to Edward Cave that he paid for the *Ramblers* even though he did not always read them. He nonetheless "spoke of them with honor," adding, "I have the vanity to think that I have procured admirers; that is to say, *readers*" (1:168–70).

8. Clifford (75–85) discusses the reception of the series. See also Reynolds and Wiles.

9. The translation is Bond's (1:44).

10. Lacan, as Gallop says, also leads us "not to a dead author, but to something more haunting, more ambiguous and disconcerting, to a fading author, one who is still precariously there, like the father in the dream" (177).

11. The "blockhead" remark is reported by Boswell (3:19). McGuffie's checklist provides some interesting evidence of the public's fascination with Johnson.

12. See for example Livingston, Castle, O'Donnell, and Lynn ("Sexual Difference").

3. A Difference in Nothing: Johnson and Derrida

1. Greene (see "Mr. Boswell" for example) has effectively questioned Boswell's accuracy and reliability. See also Pottle's attack on Greene's position and Greene's reply ("Biography").

2. In support of Bogel's assertion, one might for instance note that only one essay in Felicity Nussbaum and Laura Brown's *The New Eighteenth Century: Theory, Politics, English Literature* is deconstructive, and only one is "more than vaguely psychoanalytic," as Marshall Brown observes (566).

3. As Bannett says in her exceptionally lucid discussion, deconstruction's "apparent nihilism" is "offset" by the "advocacy of plurality, difference, and decentralization" (263–64).

4. See Derrida, *Grammatology*, esp. 141–57 and 313–16. Neel (161–65) and Norris (104–22) offer particularly helpful discussions of this idea.

5. This theme figures prominently in numbers 8, 41, 70, 78, 80, 89, 103, 107, 108, 110, 118, 120, 124, 133, 134, 135, 150, 151, 154, 161, 165, 178, 191, 196, and arguably others.

6. See Aarsleff (42–83). I have also benefitted from Aarsleff's "Language, Man, and Knowledge in the Sixteenth and Seventeenth Centuries," an unpublished series of lectures given at Princeton University in 1964. Copies are held by Princeton and the Warburg Institute.

7. These examples occur in chapter 3 of book 3, sections 2, 6, and 9.

8. Not everyone aligns Locke with a pure empiricism and correspondence theory of language. Cohen notices that "traces" of "the conventional correspondence theory of truth" "appear throughout his work," but he discounts this strain, saying it is "not strong enough to dominate [Locke's] inquiries" (42). See also Jolly, Ayers, and Lynn ("Locke's Eye").

9. Ellis also argues that "the extraordinarily poor exposition" of "the logocentric error," in "writer after writer," is related to Derrida's belatedness: "If the logocentric error were stated in any clearer way it would be far too obviously an unoriginal discovery" (37).

10. Bate's discussion of the vacuity theme in Johnson is authoritative (*Achievement*, chapter 2; the same material, somewhat condensed, appears in *Samuel Johnson*, esp. 296ff.). Hinnant very usefully discusses Johnson's acceptance of the Newtonian idea that the universe is a vacuum interrupted by matter rather than a plenum (1–10), and Squadrito discusses eighteenth-century ideas regarding the substantiality of space (124). For a revealing eighteenth-century discussion, see Law's *Inquiry into the Ideas of Space, Time, Immensity, and Eternity*, published in 1734. Grant provides an overview of the history of ideas about space from the Middle Ages to the scientific revolution.

11. See Locke's *Essay*, book 2, chapter 27, "Identity and Diver-

sity." Selby offers a useful summary of the response to Descartes' ideas.

12. In the expanding literature of deconstructive theology, the collection of Altizer et al. remains a valuable introduction (see esp. Scharlemann, "The Being of God When God is Not Being God," 79–108).

13. I am especially indebted throughout this section to Bate's chapter "The Hunger of the Imagination" (*Achievement* 63–91) and Sachs' chapter "The Art of Forgetfulness" (41–52).

4. "The Order in Which They Stand": (Re)Writing Johnson (Re)Writing

1. "Extemporaneous" and "*ad hoc*" are used by Fussell (160, 157), and "arbitrary" is Knoblauch's term ("Composing" 257). O'Flaherty sees Johnson "trying to explore" (526) the complexities of various weighty subjects in a "process of probing" (528), an endeavor which reportedly often ends in confusion and apparent vacillation. Curley also says that in his writings "thinking amounted to an act of empirical exploration" (86), and Curley in addition notes how "the very idea of travel as a process of empirical validation . . . was a dominant intellectual pattern in Georgian literature and certainly in Johnson's morality" (87). He also describes the characteristic movement of Johnson's mind as "an inductive search for tentative generalizations about the human lot" (86). Alkon refers to the "rambling, disorderly essays and poems that characterize the age of Johnson" ("Critical" 115). Pierce notes how Johnson's *Ramblers* enact a "struggle for self-understanding" (*Rambler* 134 is called "an especially fine example" of this procedure), and Pierce also observes that "this was the characteristic movement of his mind— from the particular to the general, from the psychological to the moral—and it was also the predominant rhetorical pattern of his periodical writing" (103). "Illogical" is used expansively by Greene ("'Logical Structure'" 331). O'Flaherty applies the same term specifically to Johnson's *Rambler* essays (535). Alkon also contrasts the "loose organization" of Johnson's essays to the "tight, logical"

structure of his sermons (*Johnson* 183–84, 190). Finally, "associative" and "almost Shandean" are offered by Damrosch ("Manner" 82, 88), who also refers to the essays as a "hodge-podge" (84).

2. Reynolds returned to England from Italy in October 1752, some seven months after the final *Rambler* (Leslie and Taylor 1:87).

3. To get some sense of the copiousness of these stories, see Boswell 1:61, 1:71, 1:107, 1:165–66, 1:178, 1:192, 1:203, 1:331, 1:341, 2:15–16, 2:344, 3:42–43, 4:127, and 4:214.

4. This phrase has been popularized in composition by Murray and others.

5. See Wimsatt's discussion of the reports of Johnson's conversational abilities (*Prose Style* 74–78). Sir Brooke Boothby for instance wrote that "Johnson spoke as he wrote. He would take up a topic and utter upon it a number of the The *Rambler*" (qtd. in Wimsatt 77).

6. "The Rationality of Faith" is the title of Sachs' concluding chapter in *Passionate Intelligence* (109–18). Although we travel different paths, I arrive where Sachs ends: "For Johnson true rationality and Christian faith are identical" (113).

7. See Schwartz (*Samuel Johnson*), Alkon ("Critical"), Wright, Tarbet, Trowbridge, and Knoblauch ("Coherence" and "Composing").

8. This shift is authoritatively described by Howell (259–98, 441–47).

9. The "Peripatetic Logic," Johnson says, "has been perhaps condemned without a candid trial" (Hazen 185).

10. Although there is widespread agreement that Johnson's focus as a critic is upon literature's effect, the profoundly moral nature of his judgment is sometimes understressed or neglected. See for example Keast ("Theoretical Foundations"), who usefully points to the importance of pleasure in Johnson's evaluation but does not stress that pleasure is only the necessary means to a didactic and moral end. Damrosch recognizes the "moral emphasis" (*Uses* 26) of Johnson's criticism, that he judges poetry "as a moralist" (222), but Damrosch also asserts that for Johnson "literary merit depends on two qualities, the power to delight and truth to nature" (45), a formulation which tends to underemphasize moral efficacy.

11. This overview is indebted to Howell.

12. In 1784 Johnson drew up a list of recommended reading for Rev. Astle. The list, printed by Boswell, includes both Watts' *Logick* and his *Improvement of the Mind*. See Boswell 4:311. In his preface to the *Preceptor*, Johnson suggests that the student who masters Duncan, whose work appears in the *Preceptor*, should proceed to study Watts (Hazen 185). As Alkon has observed ("Critical" 106n.28), John Collard in *The Essentials of Logic* (London, 1796) calls Watts and Duncan "the two logical writers in the highest esteem at our universities" (156). Publication records support this claim: between 1725 and 1797 at least twenty-nine editions of Watts' *Logick* appeared (and at least five adaptations), and Duncan's *Elements of Logick* went through at least eleven editions between 1748 and 1793.

13. For a discussion of Hermogenes and his use in teaching writing during Milton's day, see Clark 230–49.

14. In addition to Pierce's description of "the characteristic movement" of Johnson's mind (quoted in note 1), see also Curley's notion that "a dominant intellectual pattern in Georgian literature and certainly Johnson's morality" proceeds from "an inductive search for tentative generalizations" (86–87). Close examination of Johnson's rhetorical patterns, I believe, will not support these positions. Johnson methodically *begins* with generalizations, with what is "known."

15. See Watts, *Logick* 350. Hermogenes similarly advises the student that after presenting his opening aphorism, fact, or proverb, he should paraphrase it and "develop the significance" so the reader will grasp the starting point clearly; see Clark 179–208. Although Hume's injunction in his *Treatise of Human Nature* to "turn the subject on every side" might seem at first sight relevant to Johnson's practice, Hume's interest is investigative, not rhetorical; he is not interested in convincing readers so much as he is concerned with in finding the truth. See Richetti 41.

16. Schwartz (*Samuel Johnson*) has documented Johnson's extensive familiarity with the science of his day.

Works Cited

Aarsleff, Hans. *From Locke to Saussure: Essays on the Study of Language and Intellectual History*. Minneapolis: U of Minnesota P, 1982.

Abrams, M. H. *The Mirror and the Lamp: Romantic Theory and the Critical Tradition*. New York: Oxford UP, 1953.

———, ed. *The Norton Anthology of English Literature*. Vol. 1. New York: Norton, 1962.

Addison, Joseph, and Richard Steele. *The Spectator*. Ed. Donald Bond. 5 vols. Oxford: Oxford UP, 1965.

Alkon, Paul. "Critical and Logical Concepts of Method from Addison to Coleridge." *ECS* 5 (1971): 97–121.

———. *Samuel Johnson and Moral Discipline*. Evanston: Northwestern UP, 1967.

Altizer, T. J. J., et al., eds. *Deconstruction and Theology*. New York: Crossroad, 1982.

Atkins, Douglas. *Reading Deconstruction/Deconstructive Reading*. Lexington: UP of Kentucky, 1986.

Ayers, R. "Locke Versus Aristotle on Natural Kinds." *Journal of Philosophy* 78 (1981): 254–65.

Bannet, Eve Tavor. *Structuralism and the Logic of Dissent: Barthes, Derrida, Foucault, Lacan*. Urbana: U of Illinois P, 1989.

Barthes, Roland. "The Death of the Author." *Image, Music, Text*. Trans. Stephen Heath. New York: Hill and Wang, 1977.

Bate, Walter Jackson. *The Achievement of Samuel Johnson*. New York: Harcourt Brace, 1961.

———. *The Burden of the Past and the English Poet*. Cambridge: Harvard UP, 1970.

Works Cited

⸻. *Samuel Johnson.* New York: Harcourt, 1975.

⸻, ed. *Samuel Johnson: Essays from the* Rambler, Adventurer, *and* Idler. New Haven: Yale UP, 1968.

Baugh, Albert, et al., eds. *English Literature.* Vol. 1. New York: Appleton, 1954.

Berman, Art. *From the New Criticism to Deconstruction: The Reception of Structuralism and Post-Structuralism.* Urbana: U of Illinois P, 1988.

Blair, Hugh. *Lectures on Rhetoric and Belles Lettres.* Ed. Harold Harding. Landmarks in Rhetoric and Public Address. Carbondale: Southern Illinois UP, 1965.

Bloom, Harold. *The Anxiety of Influence: A Theory of Poetry.* New York: Oxford UP, 1973.

⸻. *The Breaking of the Vessels.* Chicago: U of Chicago P, 1982.

⸻, et al. *Deconstruction and Criticism.* New York: Continuum, 1979.

⸻. *Dr. Samuel Johnson and James Boswell.* New York: Chelsea House, 1986.

⸻. *Kabbalah and Criticism.* New York: Seabury, 1975.

⸻. *A Map of Misreading.* New York: Oxford UP, 1975.

⸻. *Poetry and Repression: Revisionism from Blake to Stevens.* New Haven: Yale UP, 1976.

⸻. *Ringers in the Tower: Studies in Romantic Tradition.* Chicago: U of Chicago P, 1971.

Bogel, Frederick. "Did you once see Johnson plain?": Reflections on Boswell's *Life* and the State of Eighteenth-Century Studies." Vance 73–93.

Bond, Donald, ed. *The Spectator.* By James Addison, Richard Steele, et al. 5 vols. Oxford: Clarendon, 1965.

Boswell, James. *Correspondence and Other Papers of James Boswell Relating to the Making of the Life of Johnson.* Ed. Marshall Waingrow. New York: McGraw, 1968.

⸻. *Life of Johnson.* Ed. George Birkbeck Hill and revised by L. F. Powell. 6 volumes. Oxford: Clarendon, 1934–50.

Brady, Frank, and W. K. Wimsatt, eds. *Samuel Johnson: Selected Poetry and Prose.* Berkeley: U of California P, 1977.

Bredvold, Louis, et al., eds. *Eighteenth-Century Poetry and Prose.* New York: Ronald, 1939.

Bronson, Bertrand. "Johnson Agonistes." *Johnson and Boswell: Three Essays.* U of California Publications in English, 3, 9 (1944): 363–98. Rpt. in *Johnson Agonistes and Other Essays.* Cambridge: Cambridge UP, 1946. 1–52.

———, ed. *Samuel Johnson: Rasselas, Poems, and Selected Prose.* New York: Holt, 1952.

Brown, Marshall. Review of *The New Eighteenth Century: Theory, Politics, and English Literature,* ed. Felicity Nussbaum and Laura Brown. *ECS* 22 (1989): 566–70.

Burke, John. "The Unknown Samuel Johnson." *The Unknown Samuel Johnson.* Ed. John Burke. Madison: U of Wisconsin P, 1983. 3–16.

———. "When the Falklands First Demanded an Historian: Johnson, Junius, and the Making of History in 1771." *The Age of Johnson* 2 (1989): 291–310.

Campbell, George. *The Philosophy of Rhetoric.* Ed. Lloyd Bitzer. Carbondale: Southern Illinois UP, 1963.

Carter, Elizabeth, and Catherine Talbot. *A Series of Letters between Mrs. Elizabeth Carter and Miss Catherine Talbot.* Ed. Montagu Pennington. 2 vols. London, 1808.

Castle, Terry. "Eros and Liberty at the English Masquerade 1710–1790." *ECS* 17 (1983/84): 156–76.

Chambers, Ephraim. *Cyclopaedia or A Universal Dictionary of Arts and Sciences.* 4th edition. 2 volumes. London, 1741.

Chapin, Chester. *The Religious Thought of Samuel Johnson.* Ann Arbor: U of Michigan P, 1968.

Chapman, R. W., ed. *Selections from Samuel Johnson.* Oxford: Oxford UP, 1962.

Clark, Donald L. *John Milton at St. Paul's School.* New York: Columbia UP, 1948.

Clifford, James. *Dictionary Johnson: Samuel Johnson's Middle Years.* New York: McGraw, 1979.

Cohen, Murray. *Sensible Words: Linguistic Practice in England 1640–1795.* Baltimore: Johns Hopkins UP, 1977.

Works Cited

Crossan, John Dominic. *Cliffs of Fall: Paradox and Polyvalence in the Parables of Jesus*. New York: Seabury, 1980.

Culler, Jonathan. *Framing the Sign: Criticism and Its Institutions*. Norman: U of Oklahoma P, 1988.

Curley, Thomas. *Samuel Johnson and the Life of Travel*. Athens: U of Georgia P, 1976.

Damrosch, Leopold. "Johnson's Manner of Proceeding in the *Rambler*." *ELH* 40 (1973): 70–89.

———. *The Uses of Johnson's Criticism*. Charlottesville: UP of Virginia, 1976.

Davis, Philip. *In Mind of Johnson: A Study of Johnson the Rambler*. London: Athlone, 1989.

De Bolla, Peter. *Harold Bloom: Towards Historical Rhetorics*. London: Routledge, 1988.

De Man, Paul. *Allegories of Reading: Figural Language in Rousseau, Nietzsche, Rilke, and Proust*. New Haven: Yale UP, 1979.

———. *Blindness and Insight: Essays in the Rhetoric of Contemporary Fiction*. New York: Oxford UP, 1971.

DeMaria, Robert. *Johnson's Dictionary and the Language of Learning*. Chapel Hill: U of North Carolina P, 1986.

———. "The Theory of Language in Johnson's *Dictionary*." *Johnson After Two Hundred Years*. Ed. Paul Korshin. Philadelphia: U of Pennsylvania P, 1986. 159–74.

Derrida, Jacques. "Deconstruction and the Other." *Dialogues with Contemporary Continental Thinkers*. Ed. Richard Kearney. Manchester: Manchester UP, 1984. 107–26.

———. "The Laws of Reflection: Nelson Mandela, in Admiration." *For Nelson Mandela*. Ed. Jacques Derrida and Mustapha Tilli. New York: Seaver, 1987. 13–42.

———. *Margins of Philosophy*. Trans. Alan Bass. Chicago: U of Chicago P, 1982.

———. *Of Grammatology*. Trans. G. C. Spivak. Baltimore: Johns Hopkins UP, 1976.

———. *Positions*. Trans. Alan Bass. Chicago: U of Chicago P, 1981.

———. "Structure, Sign, and Play in the Discourse of the Human Sciences." *The Structuralist Controversy*. Ed. Richard Macksey and Eugenio Donato, trans. by Richard Macksey. Baltimore: Johns Hopkins UP, 1970. 247–64.

———. *Writing and Difference*. Trans. Alan Bass. Chicago: U of Chicago P, 1978.

Dufrenne, Mikel. *Le poétique: précédé de 'Pour une philosophie non théologiqué*. Paris: Presses Universitaires de France, 1973.

Duncan, William. "The Elements of Logick." *The Preceptor*. Ed. Robert Dodsley. 2 vols. London, 1748. 1:9–192.

Eagleton, Terry. *Literary Theory: An Introduction*. Oxford: Blackwell, 1983.

Eco, Umberto. *Semiotics and the Philosophy of Language*. London: Macmillan, 1984.

Edinger, William. *Samuel Johnson and Poetic Style*. Chicago: U of Chicago P, 1977.

Ehrenpreis, Irvin. "*Rasselas* and Some Meanings of 'Structure' in Literary Criticism." *Novel* 14 (1981): 101–17.

Elam, Helen Regueiro. "Harold Bloom." *Modern American Critics Since 1955*. Volume 67 of the *Dictionary of Literary Biography*. Ed. Gregory Jay. Detroit: Gale, 1988. 32–48.

Elder, A. T. "Thematic Patterning and Development in Johnson's Essays." *SP* 62 (1965): 610–32.

Ellis, John. *Against Deconstruction*. Princeton: Princeton UP, 1989.

Fish, Stanley. *Is There a Text in This Class?: The Authority of Interpretive Communities*. Cambridge: Harvard UP, 1980.

Fite, David. *Harold Bloom: The Rhetoric of Romantic Vision*. Amherst: U of Massachusetts P, 1985.

Flaherty, Peter. "(Con)textual Contest: Derrida and Foucault on Madness and the Cartesian Subject." *Philosophy of the Social Sciences* 16 (1986): 157–75.

Foucault, Michel. *The Order of Things: An Archaeology of the Human Sciences*. Trans. Alan Sheridan. New York: Pantheon, 1970.

———. "What Is an Author?" *Textual Strategies: Perspectives in Post-Structuralist Criticism*. Ed. Josue V. Harari. Ithaca: Cornell UP, 1979. 141–60.

Fussell, Paul. *Samuel Johnson and the Life of Writing*. New York: Harcourt, 1971.

Works Cited

Gallop, Jane. *Reading Lacan*. Ithaca: Cornell UP, 1985. *Gentleman's Magazine*. 20 (March 1750): 126.

Gibbon, Edward. *Memoirs of My Life*. Ed. Georges A. Bonnard. London, 1866.

Goodheart, Eugene. *The Skeptic Disposition in Contemporary Criticism*. Princeton: Princeton UP, 1984.

Gould, Eric. "Deconstruction and Its Discontents." *Denver Quarterly* 15 (1980): 90–106.

Graff, Gerald. *Professing Literature: An Institutional History*. Chicago: U of Chicago P, 1987.

Grant, Edward. *Much Ado About Nothing: Theories of Space and Vacuum from the Middle Ages to the Scientific Revolution*. Cambridge: Cambridge UP, 1981.

Greene, Donald. "Boswell's *Life* as 'Literary Biography.' " Vance 161–71.

———. " 'Logical Structure' in Eighteenth-Century Poetry." *PQ* 31 (1952): 315–36.

———. *Samuel Johnson*. Twayne English Authors Series. New York: Twayne, 1970.

———, ed. *Samuel Johnson*. The Oxford Authors. Oxford: Oxford UP, 1984.

———. *Samuel Johnson: Updated Edition*. Twayne English Authors Series 95. New York: Twayne, 1989.

———. " 'Tis a Pretty Book, Mr. Boswell, But—." Vance 110–46.

Grundy, Isobel. *Samuel Johnson and the Scale of Greatness*. Athens: U of Georgia P, 1986.

———. "Samuel Johnson as Patron of Women." *The Age of Johnson* 1 (1988): 59–77.

Hagstrum, Jean. "Samuel Johnson Among the Deconstructionists." *Georgia Review* 39 (1985): 537–47. Rpt. in *Eros and Vision: The Restoration to Romanticism*. Evanston: Northwestern UP, 1989. 139–52.

Hardy, J. P. *Samuel Johnson: A Critical Study*. London: Routledge, 1979.

Harris, Roy. *The Language-Makers*. Ithaca: Cornell UP, 1980.

Hart, Kevin. *The Trespass of the Sign: Deconstruction, Theology, and Philosophy*. Cambridge: Cambridge UP, 1989.

Hartman, Geoffrey. *Criticism in the Wilderness: The Study of Literature Today*. New Haven: Yale UP, 1980.

Hawkes, Terence. *Structuralism and Semiotics*. Los Angeles: U of California P, 1977.

Hawkins, John. *The Life of Samuel Johnson, LL.D.* 1787. New York: Garland, 1974.

Hazen, Allen T., ed. *Samuel Johnson's Prefaces and Dedications*. New Haven: Yale UP, 1937.

Hibbert, Christopher. *The Personal History of Samuel Johnson*. New York: Harper, 1971.

Hill, George Birkbeck, ed. *Johnsonian Miscellanies*. 2 Vols. Oxford: Clarendon, 1897.

Hinnant, Charles. *Samuel Johnson: An Analysis*. New York: St. Martin's, 1988.

Howell, Wilbur S. *Eighteenth-Century British Logic and Rhetoric*. Princeton: Princeton UP, 1971.

Hudson, Nicholas. *Samuel Johnson and Eighteenth-Century Thought*. Oxford: Clarendon, 1988.

Jay, Gregory. *America the Scrivener: Deconstruction and the Subject of Literary History*. Ithaca: Cornell UP, 1990.

———. "Father Figures and Literary History." *T. S. Eliot and the Poetics of Literary History*. Baton Rouge and London: Louisiana State UP, 1983. 67–79.

Johnson, Samuel. *Diaries, Prayers, and Annals*. Ed. E. L. McAdam, Jr., with Donald and Mary Hyde. Vol. 1 of *The Yale Edition of the Works of Samuel Johnson*. New Haven: Yale UP, 1958.

———. *A Dictionary of the English Language*. 2 vols. London, 1755.

———. *The History of Rasselas, Prince of Abissinia*. Oxford: Oxford UP, 1968.

———. *Idler and Adventurer*. Ed. W. J. Bate, J. M. Bullitt, and L. F. Powell. Vol. 2 of *The Yale Edition of the Works of Samuel Johnson*. New Haven: Yale UP, 1963.

———. *Johnson on Shakespeare*. Ed. Arthur Sherbo. Vols. 7 and 8 of *The Yale Edition of the Works of Samuel Johnson*. New Haven: Yale UP, 1968.

———. *The Lives of the English Poets*. Ed. G. B. Hill. 3 vols. Oxford: Clarendon, 1905.

Works Cited

------. "The Plan of an English Dictionary." In Vol. 5 of *The Works of Samuel Johnson*. Oxford: Talboys and Wheeler, 1825. 1–22.

------. *Poems*. Ed. E. L. McAdam, Jr., with George Milne. Vol. 6 of *The Yale Edition of the Works of Samuel Johnson*. New Haven: Yale UP, 1965.

------. Preface. *The Preceptor*. Ed. Robert Dodsley. London, 1748. Rpt. in Hazen 171–89.

------. "Preface to the English Dictionary." In Vol. 5 of *The Works of Samuel Johnson*. Oxford: Talboys and Wheeler, 1825. 23–51.

------. *The Rambler*. Ed. W. J. Bate and Albrecht Strauss. Vols. 3, 4, and 5 of *The Yale Edition of the Works of Samuel Johnson*. New Haven: Yale UP, 1969.

------. *Sermons*. Ed. Jean Hagstrum and James Gray. Vol. 14 of the *The Yale Edition of the Works of Samuel Johnson*. New Haven: Yale UP, 1978.

Jolly, Nicholas. *Leibniz and Locke: A Study of the "New Essays on Human Understanding."* Oxford: Clarendon, 1984.

Keast, William R. "Johnson's Criticism of the Metaphysical Poets." *ELH* 17 (1950): 59–70.

------. "The Theoretical Foundations of Johnson's Criticism." *Critics and Criticism, Ancient and Modern*. Ed. R. S. Crane. Chicago: U of Chicago P, 1952. 389–407.

Kemp, Peter. "L'éthique au lendemain des victoires des athéismes: rèflexions sur la philosophie de Jacques Derrida." *Revue de théologie et de philosophie* 111 (1979): 105–21.

Kernan, Alvin. *Print Technology, Letters, and Samuel Johnson*. Princeton: Princeton UP, 1987.

Knoblauch, Cyril. "Coherence Betrayed: Samuel Johnson and 'the Prose of the World.' " *boundary 2: Revisions of the Anglo-American Tradition* (Winter 1979): 235–60.

------. "Samuel Johnson and the Composing Process." *ECS* 13 (1980): 243–62.

Korshin, Paul. " 'Johnson and . . .': Conceptions of Literary Relationship." *Greene Centennial Studies: Essays Presented to Donald Greene in the Centennial Year of the University of Southern Califor-*

nia. Ed. Paul Korshin and Robert Allen. Charlottesville: UP of Virginia, 1984. 288–306.

———. "The Paradox of Johnsonian Studies." *Johnson After Two Hundred Years*. Ed. Paul Korshin. Philadelphia: U of Pennsylvania P, 1986. ix–xix.

Kuhn, Thomas. *The Structure of Scientific Revolutions*. 2nd ed. Chicago: U of Chicago P, 1970.

Law, William. *An Inquiry into the Ideas of Space, Time, Immensity, and Eternity*. Cambridge, 1734.

Leslie, Charles Robert, and Tom Taylor. *Life and Times of Sir Joshua Reynolds*. 2 vols. London, 1865.

Livingston, Chella. "Samuel Johnson and the Role of Women." Diss. U of South Carolina, 1985.

Locke, John. *An Essay Concerning Human Understanding*. Ed. Peter Nidditch. Oxford: Clarendon, 1975.

Lynn, Steven. "Johnson's *Rambler* and Eighteenth-Century Rhetoric." *ECS* 19 (1986): 461–79.

———. "Locke's Eye, Adam's Tongue, Johnson's Word: Language, Marriage, and 'The Choice of Life.' " *The Age of Johnson* 3 (1990): 35–61.

———. "Sexual Difference and Johnson's Brain." Nath 123–49.

Magliola, Robert. *Derrida on the Mend*. West Lafayette: Purdue UP, 1984.

McGuffie, Helen Louise. *Samuel Johnson in the British Press, 1749–1784: A Chronological Checklist*. New York: Garland, 1976.

Miller, J. Hillis. *The Ethics of Reading*. The Wellek Library Lectures 5. New York: Columbia UP, 1987.

Minsky, Marvin. "The Intelligence Transplant." *Discover* 10 (1989): 52–59.

Montagu, Mary Wortley. *The Complete Letters of Lady Mary Wortley Montagu*. Ed. Robert Halsband. 3 vols. Oxford: Oxford UP, 1967.

Moore, Cecil. *English Prose of the Eighteenth Century*. New York: Holt, 1933.

Murphy, Arthur. "An Essay on the Life and Genius of Samuel Johnson, LL.D." Hill 1:353–488.

Murray, Donald. *A Writer Teaches Writing*. Boston: Houghton, 1968.

Works Cited

Nath, Prem, ed. *Fresh Reflections on Samuel Johnson: Essays in Criticism*. Troy: Whitston, 1987.

Neel, Jasper. *Plato, Derrida, and Writing*. Carbondale: Southern Illinois UP, 1988.

Norris, Christopher. *Derrida*. Cambridge: Harvard UP, 1987.

O'Donnell, Sheryl Rae. "'Born to Know, Reason, and to Act': Samuel Johnson's Attitude Toward Women as Reflected in His Writings." Diss. U of Arizona, 1979.

O'Flaherty, Patrick. "Towards an Understanding of Johnson's *Rambler*." *SEL* 18 (1978): 523–36.

Olson, Robert. *Motto, Context, Essay: The Classical Background of Samuel Johnson's* Rambler *and* Adventurer *Essays*. New York: UP of America, 1984.

Ong, Walter. "The Writer's Audience is Always a Fiction." *Interfaces of the Word: Studies in the Evolution of Consciousness and Culture*. Ithaca: Cornell UP, 1977. 53–81.

Pemberton, Henry. *A View of Sir Isaac Newton's Philosophy*. Dublin, 1728.

Percy, Bishop. "Anecdotes and Remarks." *Johnsonian Miscellanies*. Ed. G. B. Hill. 2 vols. Oxford: Clarendon, 1897. 2:208–18.

Pierce, Charles. *The Religious Life of Samuel Johnson*. Hamden: Archon, 1983.

Piozzi, Hester Thrale. *Anecdotes of the Late Samuel Johnson*. Rpt. in *Johnsonian Miscellanies*. Ed. G. B. Hill. 2 vols. Oxford: Clarendon, 1897. 1:141–352.

Pottle, Frederick. "The Adequacy as Biography of Boswell's *Life of Johnson*." Vance 147–60.

Price, John. *The Ironic Hume*. Austin: U of Texas P, 1965.

Radner, John. "The Significance of Johnson's Changing Views of the Hebrides." *The Unknown Samuel Johnson*. Ed. John Burke and Donald Kay. Madison: U of Wisconsin P, 1983. 131–49.

Raschke, Carl. "The Deconstruction of God." Altizer et al. 1–33.

Reynolds, W. V. "The Reception of Johnson's Prose Style." *RES* 11 (1935): 145–62.

Richardson, Samuel. *The Correspondence of Samuel Richardson*. Ed. Anna Laetitia Barbauld. 6 vols. London, 1804.

Richetti, John. *Philosophical Writing: Locke, Berkeley, Hume*. Cambridge: Harvard UP, 1983.

Riddel, Joseph. "Juda Becomes New Haven." *Diacritics* 10 (Summer 1980): 17–34.

Riely, J. C. "The Pattern of Imagery in Johnson's Periodical Essays." *ECS* 3 (1970): 384–97.

Roberts, William. *The Looker-On, A Periodical Paper*. London, 1795.

Rogers, Katherine. *Feminism in Eighteenth-Century England*. Urbana: U of Illinois P, 1982.

Rogers, Pat. *The Augustan Vision*. New York: Barnes, 1974.

Rogers, Samuel. *Recollections of the Table-Talk of Samuel Rogers*. Ed. A. Dyce. London, 1856.

Ruf, Henry, ed. *Religion, Ontotheology, and Deconstruction*. New York: Paragon, 1989.

Sachs, Arieh. *Passionate Intelligence*. Baltimore: Johns Hopkins UP, 1967.

Scharlemann, Robert. "The Being of God When God is Not Being God." Altizer et al. 79–108.

Schneidau, Herbert. *Sacred Discontent: The Bible and Western Tradition*. Berkeley: U of California P, 1976.

Schwartz, Richard. "Johnson's 'Mr. Rambler' and the Periodical Tradition." *Genre* 7 (1974): 196–204.

———. *Samuel Johnson and the New Science*. Madison: U of Wisconsin P, 1971.

Selby, Hopewell. "'Never Finding Full Repast': Satire and Self-Extension in the Early Eighteenth Century." *Probability, Time, and Space in Eighteenth-Century Literature*. Ed. Paula Backsheider. New York: AMS, 1979. 141–66.

Selden, Raman. "Deconstructing the *Ramblers*." Nath 269–82.

Sheriff, John. *The Fate of Meaning: Charles Pierce, Structuralism, and Literature*. Princeton: Princeton UP, 1989.

Siebert, Donald. "Johnson and Hume on Miracles." *JHI* 36 (1975): 543–47.

Spivak, Gayatri. "Translator's Preface." *Of Grammatology*. By Jacques Derrida. Baltimore: Johns Hopkins UP, 1976. ix–xc.

Squadrito, Kathleen. *John Locke*. Twayne English Authors Series 271. New York: Twayne, 1979.

Works Cited

Steele, Richard. *The Guardian*. Philadelphia: Woodward, 1831.

Stuart, Reid. *The Essays of Samuel Johnson: Selections from* The Rambler, The Adventurer, and The Idler. London: Walter Scott, 1883.

Tarbet, David. "Lockean 'Intuition' and Johnson's Characterization of Aesthetic Response." *ECS* 1 (1971): 58–79.

Taylor, Mark. *Deconstructing Theology*. New York: Crossroad, 1982.

Trowbridge, Hoyt. "Scattered Atoms of Probability." *ECS* 5 (1971): 1–38.

Vance, John, ed. *Boswell's* Life of Johnson: *New Questions, New Answers*. Athens: U of Georgia P, 1985.

Voitle, Robert. *Samuel Johnson the Moralist*. Cambridge: Harvard UP, 1961.

Wain, John. *Samuel Johnson*. New York: Viking, 1975.

Walsh, Thomas. "Deconstruction, Countersecularization, and Communicative Action: Prelude to Metaphysics." Ruf 114–26.

Wasserman, Earl. "Johnson's *Rasselas*: Implicit Contexts." *JEGP* 74 (1975): 1–25.

Watts, Isaac. *Logick; or, the Right Use of Reason in the Inquiry After Truth*. London, 1740.

———. *Philosophical Essays on Various Subjects*. London, 1742.

Weinbrot, Howard. "Masked Men and Satire and Pope: Toward a Historical Basis for the Eighteenth-Century Persona." *ECS* 16 (1983): 265–89.

Wharton, T. F. *Samuel Johnson and the Theme of Hope*. London: Macmillan, 1984.

White, James Boyd. *When Words Lose Their Meanings: Constitutions and Reconstitutions of Language, Character, and Community*. Chicago: U of Chicago P, 1984.

Wiles, R. M. "The Contemporary Distribution of Johnson's *Rambler*." *ECS* 2 (1968): 155–71.

Wimsatt, W. K. *Philosophic Words*. New Haven: Yale UP, 1948.

———. *The Prose Style of Samuel Johnson.* New Haven: Yale UP, 1941.

Worden, John. "The Themes and Techniques of Johnson's *Rambler*." Diss. U of Southern California, 1971.

Wright, John W. "Samuel Johnson and Traditional Methodology." *PMLA* 86 (1971): 40–50.

Index

Aarsleff, Hans, 80, 86
Abrams, M. H., 7
Absence, 92
Adamic language, 80–81, 83–85
Addison, Joseph: allusions to, 22–37; criticism of Milton, 46–49; goal of *The Spectator*, 39, 58; method of composing, 121; popularity of, 2, 42, 43; women, depictions of, 44, 53–55, 59–60
Aldrich, Dean, 139
Alkon, Paul, 8, 116
Allegory, 39
Almamoulin, 111
Anthea, 46
Anxiety of influence, 25
Arbitrariness, 147
Aristotle, 138–39
Atkins, Douglas, 96
Aurelia, 59
Author, 51, 57, 87
Author's task, 126

Bacon, Sir Francis, 27
Baker, Thomas, 88–89
Bate, Walter Jackson: Johnson and modern thought, 19–68; Johnson as outcast, 13; relationship of *The Rambler* to *The Spectator*, 24–25; selection of *Rambler* essays, 6–8; themes in *The Rambler*, 27, 137; unevenness of *The Rambler*, 9–10
Baugh, Albert, 7
Beginning, the problem of, 35–36

Belief, 110, 159–61
Bellaria, 54
Berman, Art, 73, 82
Bible, 19–20
Black holes, 94
Blackmore, Richard, 155
Blair, Hugh, 82–84, 140
Bloom, Harold: deconstruction, 99; metalepsis, 35; misreading of Johnson, 61–64, 158; negation, 46; Oedipal conflict, 61–64; rhetoric as defense, 19, 25–28, 29, 36, 41, 44, 51–52
Bogel, Frederick, 68–69
Bond, Donald, 49–50
Borges, Jorge Luis, 80
Boswell, James: composing, Johnson's method of, 116, 118–21; context of *The Rambler*, 21–26; conversation, Johnson's aim in, 125; "Dr. Johnson," 3, 52, 63; Hawkins, as competitor, 21–24; rhetorical strategies, 29, 121, 165n.6; title of *The Rambler*, 10–12; variety of *The Rambler*, 13, 99
Boyle, Robert, 81
Bredvold, Louis, 7
Bronson, Bertrand, 6, 69
Burke, John, 3, 161
Bustle, Lady, 54
Bute, Countess of, 24

Camilla, 58
Campbell, George, 82–84, 140
Carter, Elizabeth, 24

187

Index

Index

Steven Lynn is an associate professor of English at the University of South Carolina. His interests include eighteenth-century literature, the history of rhetoric, and critical theory.